ALL ABOUT
WINE
CELLARS

ALL ABOUT
WINE
CELLARS

by Howard G. Goldberg

RUNNING PRESS
PHILADELPHIA · LONDON

9   8   7   6   5   4   3   2   1
Digit on the right indicates the number of this printing

Library of Congress Control Number: 2002095664

ISBN 0-7624-1557-6

Cover and interior design by Corinda Cook
Edited by Lynn Rosen
Photo Research by Susan Oyama
Typography: Caslon, Calisto, Minister, and Arabesque Ornament

Photography Credits:
Slipcase left to right: Michael Weiss; CMI/Picture24/Bach/Robertstock.com; CEPHAS/Diana Mewes; CEPHAS/Mick Rock
Slipcase back cover: Michael Weiss
Front book cover and p. 99: CMI/Picture24/Bach/Robertstock.com
Back book cover and pp. 27, 48, 63, 71: Corbis
p. 7: CEPHAS/Pierre Hussenot
p. 12: CEPHAS/Diana Mewes
p. 37: CEPHAS/Steven Morris
pp. 50, 111: CEPHAS/Ian Shaw
p. 55: *Flowers, Fruit and Champagne* by Jean Francois Raffaelli (1850–1924). Fine Art Photographic Library, London/Art Resource, NY
pp. 79, 86, 90, 95, 103, 107: CEPHAS/Mick Rock

This book may be ordered by mail from the publisher. Please include $2.50 for postage and handling.
But try your bookstore first!

Running Press Book Publishers
125 South Twenty-second Street
Philadelphia, Pennsylvania 19103-4399

Visit us on the web!
www.runningpress.com

Upstairs, Downstairs

For a Christmas issue, *Decanter* magazine in London asked a number of its wine writers, myself included, to list what wine gifts they would most like to receive on the holiday. The answer was easy.

I am a passionate lover of riesling, the great white German grape and wine, and my favorite producer—not only in Germany but in all the world—is Maximin Grünhaus in the Ruwer Valley of the Mosel-Saar-Ruwer region. The owner, Dr. Carl-Ferdinand von Schubert, a gracious man with an elegant Old World manner, makes inexpressibly subtle dry, semidry and sweet wines from riesling planted in his vineyards, the Abtsberg, Bruderberg and Herrenberg, all contiguous on one awesome slate-filled slope. Given the opportunity, I would drink Maximin Grünhäuser wines every day of the year. It was a no-brainer to write that, as a gift, I would like Dr. von Schubert to give me my own private key to his winery's deep, cool cellar, so that I could come and go as I pleased, without interfering with the family in its villa upstairs, and could open any bottle I fancied.

The following September, when I next encountered Dr. von Schubert, at a vintage tasting in Manhattan sponsored by the German Wine Information Bureau, as usual I stopped at his table first. He greeted me warmly, reached into his pocket, took out his own keys and handed them to me. "Your keys," he said. A wonderful gesture. I accepted them symbolically. What embryonic wine collector—or, for that matter, veteran collector—wouldn't like to be handed a key to another's cellar (including a producer's cellar) and to have a free hand in selecting and opening bottles?

Collecting goes hand in hand with sharing. Given the stratospheric price of Burgundy, when Burgundy collectors invite you to carry a bottle or two from their cellars up to their dining rooms the act resembles philanthropy (alas, not the kind that is tax-deductible).

Sharing can be even more generous. One memorable August, when a professional couple, eager to escape the Roman heat, offered to entrust their small villa above the Janiculum to my wife, Beatrice, and me, one lure was the cavernous wine cellar under their spacious backyard. Entered, as if in a Gothic novel, by a creaky metal door in a courtyard wall half hidden by vegetation, the cellar—damp, moldy, cold—occupied a catacomb that much earlier had been gentrified.

Our host told us that he drove to the Tuscan estate of a favorite winemaker annually, filled the car with magnums, chiefly reds, drove home and stacked the big bottles horizontally in the catacomb for a year's consumption. "Drink as much as you would like," he said, with typical Italian generosity. We did, although I felt spooked every time I visited the cave.

As villa sitters, our sole duties were to keep the property locked—the ultra-leftist Red Brigades were rampant at the time—and to feed our hosts' two dogs, German shepherds. The owners left ample supplies of the dogs' basic menus: pasta, which was cooked daily, and meat, which would be defrosted and prepared. The older dog was not averse to an occasional dish of vino rosso, lapping it up eagerly as he wolfed down the pasta. (He showed no interest in vino bianco, which I thought was a defect in his aesthetic judgment.)

Since Italy is one vast vineyard from top to boot, it is not surprising that the nation's pets, like its children, take rations of wine in stride. From time immemorial, Mediterranean cultures have bred an ease about wine's role in daily life that sophisticated Americans, for whom wine and its lore create anxieties, can only envy.

In American wine life, what gets sidelined is old-fashioned taken-for-granted down-the-hatch pleasure, the kind you get from steak and fries or, more simply, a great rotisserie chicken. That's why I wish that for wine purposes (and a few others) Americans could also be Italian or French.

A Paris-born woman, the mother of a brood and wife of a wine distributor, described to me, at a bring-your-own-bottle dinner at Restaurant Daniel in Manhattan, how as she grew up, droplets, then small glasses, then full glasses of wine were given to her at lunch and dinner. After such an education, she said, she cannot conceive of wine as a big deal. Similarly, she is training her kids not to make a federal case out of it.

As a civilized social lubricant, wine is unequaled (despite the contrived hilarity in beer-ad partying); more rewardingly, as a deeply personal pleasure it is rivaled by reading, art and music.

Christine Hawley, who custom-designs wine cellars and uses her own crafts-men, is a keen observer of the effects of wine enthusiasm on her clients. She does only three or four cellars a year. They cost about $1 million each. "I handpick my clients, and I like to get close to them," she said.

Ms. Hawley, the wife of Michael Aaron, chairman of Sherry-Lehmann, the great wine shop on the East Side of Manhattan—he is perhaps the best-known wine merchant in America—finds that wine collecting can "provide entry into a world in which one becomes a connoisseur of life."

Her cellars are located, among many places, on Park Avenue in Manhattan; Southampton, on the South Fork of Long Island's gold coast; in Sarasota and Orlando, Florida; Minneapolis; Anguilla, in the British West Indies; Millbrook, New York, in tony Dutchess County; and Pebble Beach, California.

A subterranean cellar, called the Enoteca, that Ms. Hawley designed for a luxurious condominium building, The Loft, in the trendy SoHo neighborhood of Lower Manhattan, has attracted considerable attention. It offers all the dwellers a 2,500-square-foot wine cellar with separate storage facilities that can accommodate from 700 to 3,500 bottles. The taupe, stucco tasting room, 22 feet long, has a vaulted ceiling, wood-burning limestone fireplace, an antique-copper rinsing sink that functions as a place to chill white wines and a table that seats 16. The owners can use the room for dinner parties.

"When my clients start working with me on the plans to design their dream wine cellar, I always enjoy watching a lovely transformation come over them," Ms. Hawley said. "The process of designing and building a cellar always changes their lifestyle and begins to add new and wonderful pleasures they never before explored. It's like having a baby. People get so energized and focused.

"For instance, holiday travel suddenly sounds more exciting, with thoughts of touring wine-producing regions or possibly flying to France to visit a First

Growth chateau in Bordeaux rather than sitting on yet another sandy beach in the Bahamas. Maybe even bicycling through the vineyards or traveling on a barge through wine country. Some clients have gone so far as to participate in the harvesting of the grapes.

"Clients discover that the more they learn about wine, the more they realize how much more there is to know. Many enroll in wine tasting classes. Kevin Zraly's Windows on the World Wine School here in New York City seems to be the most popular and most exciting.

"Many customers start going to auctions. And daily dining suddenly takes on new meaning. Now, each meal is important. The menu suddenly becomes a major topic and is usually discussed in great detail. Meals provide an exciting opportunity to open a bottle or two for comparison. They also become a learning tool to discover how the wines are developing, and people have fun learning how to pair wine with food.

"My clients have seen their circles of friends change. When a very special wine is being served with a special meal, it is most enjoyable to share it with friends who appreciate the treasures being poured. Many have joined wine societies. These groups schedule amazing dinners and wonderful selections of wines.

"Birthdays reflect the new passion for collecting and consumption. Clients no longer get excited over receiving a gift from Barneys or Bergdorf—just another Hermès tie. But they do get excited when a package arrives from a fine-wine shop. Could it be a treasured First Growth from their birth year? A Riedel decanter? A sterling silver decanting funnel? A magnum of Taittinger Comtes de Champagne Blanc de Blancs?"

A Beloved Word

Except for the word "wine," no term in winedom is more pregnant with mystery, expectation and pleasure than "cellar." Its sound is resonant and its imagery rich with different sets of associations for vintners and for buyers.

A professor, Ralph C. Wood, writing about J.R.R. Tolkien, author of *Lord of the Rings*, said: "Though Tolkien's imagination was supremely visual, he would realize his images primarily in words rather than pictures. He was drawn to the sound of words no less than their meaning. He would observe that 'cellar door' is a gorgeous phrase, far more attractive than the word 'sky,' and even more beautiful than the word 'beauty' itself."

In the wine world, the word surrounds you: Wine originates in a cellar (the winery's) and spends its days in one (yours).

The word "cellar" denotes both the storage space and its contents. If you are an American Francophile, using the French word without sounding pretentious you can now freely call your cellar a cave (pronounced kahv), which means cellar or underground vault as well as a collection of wine bottles.

The word is also used casually to denote temperature- and humidity-controlled glass-fronted wine-storage units in wooden cabinets, like, most famously, EuroCaves, which increasingly are found in upscale habitats.

During transactions, salesmen at places like Sherry-Lehmann and Zachys, a sprawling emporium in affluent Scarsdale in suburban Westchester County, New York, routinely speak of their establishments' cellars. The term, in such over-the-counter instances, tends to be functionally more nearly synonymous with "warehouses."

According to Ken Collura, the head sommelier, Bern's Steak House in Tampa, Florida, has 500,000 bottles in its cellar; this may well translate into the largest restaurant wine cellar in the world. Bern's has some 6,500 wines listed on its wine cards. Some of the underpinnings: 20 vintages of La Tâche from the Domaine de la Romanée-Conti, 21 of Château Cheval Blanc, 34 of Mouton-Rothschild, 30 of Latour, 44 of Lafite-Rothschild and 36 of Haut-Brion. As for California standouts: 12 vintages of Dominus and 13 vintages of Opus One. Why not drop in one evening and open five or six?

When wine stewards and waiters in restaurants like Sparks, the great midtown Manhattan steakhouse, a virtual men's club for shirt-and-suspenders Wall Streeters, speak of the cellar, it is literally downstairs and jammed with 255,000 bottles.

By contrast, when Julian Niccolini and Alex von Bidder, part owners and managers of the elegant Four Seasons Restaurant in Manhattan, refer to their 12,000-plus bottle cellar, it is not physically in the cellar of the landmark Seagram Building, on Park Avenue: some of its handsome wooden racks are visible at eye level as guests enter the elegant, spacious Pool Room.

Then, of course, there was the wonderful Cellar in the Sky, a restaurant-within-in-a-restaurant at Windows on the World, which terrorists destroyed on 9/11. It offered one of New York's first wine-and-food-pairing menus (advertised weekly in *The New York Times*). Its wine list, at the outset, was put together by an ambitious young Kevin Zraly.

Sophisticated wine producers like Pellegrini Vineyards and Paumanok Vineyards, both on the North Fork of Long Island—the fastest-rising wine region east of the Mississippi (with the Finger Lakes of upstate New York close behind)—sometimes speak of their wine "libraries." This noun carries the general meaning of cellar, but also the specialized implication of a section of it that

houses bottles from successive vintages that are no longer commercially available but are opened only on special occasions or to learn something retrospectively about the houses' early winemaking.

In the auction world, a common axiom is: It takes two bidders to make a market. Similarly, by the most liberal but uncommon definition, it takes two bottles to make a cellar: one bottle for tonight, and one for tomorrow night, with each one being replaced the next day.

I do not, for one moment, believe that any Englishman listed in Debrett's Peerage and Baronetage would swallow this brash American notion. In his mind, a cellar would be associated with generations of claret downstairs dating from the Empire, and oil paintings of gentlemen, grouse-hunters and horsemen all, lining the polished woodwork on the second-floor balcony. But since America does not have a House of Lords, a cellar here is what we say it is. Peers of the realm whose butlers tippled from opened claret, then watered the wine to hide their habit, would have appreciated a new 21st-century gadget: a combination-lock stopper that, plugged into the bottle, prevents access.

Do you own only the industrial-strength black metal lattice racks seen in liquor stores, and stock them regularly? That's a cellar.

If you own rudimentary pine Modularacks from Australia that assemble in a flash and can store 24 bottles, that's a cellar.

A bachelor in a studio can call his seven bottles a cellar. For just-marrieds, a cellar can be merely a much-used six-bottle wooden bin in a dining alcove that they keep filled with weekly purchases.

In common parlance and in weekend newspapers' real estate articles, "wine cellar" summons images of a fancy custom-designed chamber—nay, cathedral—chockablock with scores, hundreds, even thousands, of costly laid-down bottles filling walls of lattice-like wooden shelves.

If you ascend to inexpensive electrically powered stand-alone wine coolers; or higher, to such coolers placed in elegant cabinetry; or even higher, to whole cellar rooms turned baronial with chandeliers and haute-couture carpentry; or, stratospherically, to half a warehouse floor for your holdings, you have a cellar by any definition.

Your cellar does not limit your holdings to wine acquired only for unloading in the secondary market, and to wines slumbering for decades in order, one golden day, to reveal their best selves for a fleeting moment amid guests' ooh's and aah's.

Rather, your cellar embraces wine bought for Monday night, when you're dead tired and you welcome a rustic red; for Saturday night, for a dining room dinner party at which the conversation flows like chamber music; for Sunday, to lubricate a wedding; and for something nebulous, typically called the middle term, which means loosely five years off.

The Nitty-Gritty

Why create and organize a wine cellar—that is, a fully controlled manmade environment?

Because, as in all issues involving personal independence, it is desirable not to have to rely unduly on outsiders—in this instance, the wine inventory of neighborhood retailers or, if you live in a legally enlightened American state, supermarkets.

If you buy studiously and at leisure, focusing on wines for immediate, medium- and long-term drinking, you control all the serving conditions. You are less likely to overpay for a bottle, or wind up disappointed because one is unready for drinking or over the hill, which can happen as a result of a rush visit to a store en route home from work.

In addition, you can draw on a careful selection of wines for any occasion, whether for a new recipe, a special dinner, a party at which guests express a preference for certain wines, or gift giving. Cellars enable you to save money by large-scale purchases, which usually entail discounts; by buying during sales and when futures are offered; by jumping in when an especially desirable vintage is released and before shortages of it set in.

Then there are the pleasures of connoisseurship, aesthetics, accumulation, possession—all to be shared with family, friends, neighbors, colleagues and business associates.

But, to be grumpy for a moment, cellars can have downsides, too. Technicians can be hired to design and build one without your input, and commissioned wine consultants can furnish the bottles, much as the picture-perfect rooms in shelter magazines may be wholly fitted out by interior designers. But such McMansion showpiece cellars exist primarily to flaunt economic and social status—what the social scientist Thorstein Veblen called "conspicuous consumption"—and thus are spiritually empty. They smack of the smarmy messages implied in too many wine ads: "Impress the boss. Outdo the neighbors." A real cellar, in my view, arises primarily from a love of the thing in itself, like a garden, not from a love of showing it off. It's the difference between having a real wife and an—ugh—trophy wife.

There are the semi-parental satisfactions of collecting, of nursing wines from youth through maturity, of steadily enjoying the stages of development of their personal characteristics. By thoughtful planning and nurturing, you carefully rear great wine, protecting it, insofar as it is possible, from going bad in the bottle because of unsuitable external conditions.

If you have bought, say, two cases of Château Mouton-Rothschild, a First Growth from Bordeaux, from the celebrated 2000 vintage and open a bottle every year, you will have 24 years of drinking, 24 years of notes that carefully trace the wine's evolution—its time line, as the wine trade calls it. This is roughly akin to returning to Shakespeare's *Hamlet* annually, in each round of reading discovering hitherto unappreciated themes, depths and other elusive satisfactions available to mature minds.

Investment for ultimate resale and profitability adds a further reward. Focused buyers can drink great wine free by judiciously acquiring two cases instead of one. As they consume the first, they watch prices rise for the second, and, at exactly the right time, dispose of the second case at a profit so substantial that it covers the costs of drinking the first. This is about as close to free lunch as it gets in the wine world, or anywhere else for that matter.

Jeffersonian Vinocracy

Perhaps the most distinguished cellar in the Republic's infancy was amassed by Thomas Jefferson, whom many consider the most intellectually curious and gifted of America's 43 presidents.

As John F. Kennedy said at a dinner for Nobel Prize winners in 1962, "I think this is the most extraordinary collection of talent, of human knowledge, that has ever been gathered together at the White House, with the possible exception of when Thomas Jefferson dined alone."

Katherine G. Revell, a researcher, in a 1996 document prepared under the direction of Susan R. Stein, curator for the Thomas Jefferson Memorial Foundation at Monticello, Virginia, wrote: Jefferson's wine stock was so valuable that he kept it under double locks in the dining room cellar at Monticello.

"Jefferson gained a reputation during his lifetime as a wine connoisseur, and advised Washington, Adams, Madison and Monroe on stocking their wine cellars," Ms. Revell wrote. "During his own tenure as president, he sought to expand the taste of his dinner guests, who often commented on the high quality of the wines served at the president's house.

"Guests sampled Champagne and wines from some of the most well-known wine houses of France, including Château Margaux and Hermitage, as well as lesser-known wines from southern France, Spain and Italy. This scale of hospitality cost Jefferson considerable expense, spending a third of his $25,000 annual salary on food and drink during his first year in office.

"Although no description of the arrangement of wine racks, bins, or storage methods in the dining room cellar at Monticello has been recovered to date,

Jefferson took notes on cellar bottle arrangements in two cellars in France" during his diplomatic service there, the Revell document said. "Although no cellar book has been recovered, Jefferson inventoried his wine stock from time to time and also kept track of his stock of empty bottles." Fragments of bottles and wine bottle seals have been found at Monticello.

Even as today's cellar owners record their tasting notes in their computers or in cellar books, "Jefferson took notes on the wines he drank" during his European travels in 1787 and 1788. "His travels took him to Burgundy, the Rhône Valley, Nîmes, Turin, Milan, Genoa, Nice, Provence, Languedoc, as well as Bordeaux, Holland, the Rhine Valley and Champagne," Ms. Revell wrote.

Jefferson's sophistication was such that in retirement, when reduced financial circumstances "may have forced him to make compromises in quality as he chose wine for Monticello," instead of buying Champagne, Jefferson ordered a "dry, spirituous blanquette de Limoux made near Carcassonne." In addition, "he now relied on Henry Bergasse of Marseilles to create a blended vin rouge for household use, which Jefferson described as 'so perfect an imitation of the finest Bordeaux as not to be distinguishable.'"

Making a Cellar

Imagine a mini-world of trellised pigeonholes, cubes, rectangles, diamonds, curved corners, waterfall forms, in staggered heights (some needing a stepladder or a stool), with shelves for wooden cases and cardboard boxes, possibly drawers, everything neatly flush against walls or extending into the room, creating niches for bottles, bottles and more bottles, all centered on a table top for tasting and writing notes, and graced with crystal ware hanging upside down from slats.

The dream of filling sections of a room, or better yet a whole room, from its terra-cotta-colored tile floor to its ceiling, with wine-enclosed wood arouses our sense of pleasurable expectation. But not all wood is equal to all other wood, and here is where the lessons start pouring in.

Because of the high and sustained humidity levels in proper cellars, only woods that are mildew- and decay-resistant should be chosen to fashion the shelves and molding. Honduran mahogany, so-called all-heart redwood, red oak and Georgian pecan serve cellar designs well. (Though critics occasionally recommend cedar, a very popular wood, that is an error. Cedar is better suited for clothing closets; its heavy aroma may penetrate wine corks and destroy flavor.)

Creating a cellar when a house is being built or remodeled, or when a city apartment is being redone, is a major undertaking. It requires full-scale advance planning and, prudently, an elastic budget (prepare for a potential cost overrun) that contemplates an architect, a designer and other contractors customarily involved in construction (backhoe operator, materials suppliers, engineer, electrician, plumber, carpenter, air-conditioning technician, etc.). Some experts recommend that you start planning a year in advance of the hoped-for day of completion. The smart money chooses experienced contractors who specialize in wine cellars rather than general contractors, no matter how glowing their reputations.

No rush jobs, please. Every last detail must be envisioned properly beforehand; otherwise, heartache, oversights and expensive remedial action will surely follow. This is especially true if you are shunning outside professionals in favor of a do-it-yourself project that involves kits.

What self-reliant adult exposed in childhood to an Erector Set, Lincoln Logs or Legos could resist the do-it-yourself architectural and design lures of wooden racks? It is not, as they say, rocket science: all you need is a carpenter's ruler and a calculator. If you have a software program that enables you to create multidimensional designs on your computer, so much the better.

To realize this dream, before ordering a custom-wine-cellar kit from a catalog house (whose staff may offer guidance, including design assistance) you need a carefully worked out step-by-step plan for storage of a predetermined number of bottles of various sizes, with everything predicated on careful measurements so that when the materials arrive everything fits.

Short of visiting collectors and showrooms, the best way to understand, to derive lessons from, the appearances, layouts, furnishings, ambience and contents of personal cellars is to solicit literature from veteran manufacturers and installers.

Names can be found in the classified advertisements in the indispensable *Wine Spectator*. Incidentally, this 18-times-a-year consumer-oriented magazine, published by Marvin R. Shanken, president of Shanken Communications, in New York, is the ultimate American desert-island publication for wine novices and cognoscenti alike. In words and photographs, and importantly in its advertising, over time it provides boundless mini and maxi ideas about cellar acquisition, development and management.

A tough businessman with vision, and a philanthropist, Shanken may be appreciated historically as a giant late-20th-century and early-21st-century force in cultivating and elevating Americans' taste for wine. His motives may be mainly commercial, but their profoundly civilizing effects have improved innumerable lives.

Here is a list of cellar-preparing professionals to keep in mind. They have done out-of-state work. Though the list, presented alphabetically, is by no means comprehensive, it is select.

Apex
13221 Northup Way
Bellevue, Washington 98005
(www.apexwinecellars.com; ask about regional offices)

Christine Hawley Designs
155 West 70th Street
New York, New York 10023
(no Web site; chawley@adiglobal.com)

Fine Wine Rack and Cellar Company (Paul Wyatt Designs)
512 Technology Way
Napa, California 94558
(www.paulwyatt.com)

Kedco
564 Smith Street
Farmingdale, Long Island, New York 11735-1168

New England Wine Cellars

Post Office Box 257

West Cornwall, Connecticut 06796

(www.newcellars.com)

Wine Cellar Concepts

6800 Fleetwood Road

McLean, Virginia 22101

(www.winecellarconcepts.com)

Wine Cellar Innovations (formerly Wine Racks Unlimited)

4575 Eastern Avenue

Cincinnati, Ohio 45226

(www.winecellarinnovations.com)

The catalogs from two-large scale mail-order houses that dominate the commercial winescape, *The Wine Enthusiast* (www.wineenthusiast.com) and IWA, or *International Wine Accessories* (www.iwawine.com), offer various cellar services.

To get a sense of what superior—indeed, top-of-the-line—craftsmanship looks and feels like and is likely to cost, visit especially the Web site of Paul Wyatt Designs and meet, in virtual reality, its proprietor, who has spent two decades thinking about the large aesthetic and engineering problems and tiny details that go into super-intelligent wine storage.

Yes, many Wyatt cellars shown have art gallery, boardroom and palatial appearances: there is no escaping (who would want to?) the ravishing multilevel designs and details, especially the curved corners and curved racks, exquisite indirect lighting and graceful Romanesque and Gothic arches and archways that affluence can command.

I would not disagree with Wyatt's observation that the wine cellars he develops "are places of beauty that, like the wines they hold, transcend their simple materials," and I only marginally disagree with his position that his "showcases are as prestigious and impressive as the wines that reside there."

The England-born Wyatt's clients, found on many continents, have included Copia, the American Center for Wine, Food and the Arts, in Napa, California; Cakebread Cellars, in Rutherford, California; the Ferrari-Carano winery, in Healdsburg, California; Masa's Restaurant, in San Francisco, and, his client list says, "chief executive officers, chief financial officers, royalty, heads of state." His prices for designing, constructing and assembling cellars have ranged from tens of thousands to hundreds of thousands of dollars.

"If you have a big wine cellar," Wyatt said, "it means you are a nice guy and sociable and accepted by your fellow man, which is nice, isn't it? And maybe you'll even be chosen head of the tribe."

The Web site (and mailed literature) of Wine Cellars Innovations is no less impressive to amble through, though it radiates less exclusivity and refinement than does Wyatt's. The company's founder and chief executive officer, Jim Deckebach, has assembled an impressive array of custom-design goodies to show what is available to the collector who wants pretty much everything. Check out the etched and painted cellar entry doors; the "quarter round display cabinet," which "make a dramatic, sweeping transition on outside corners between straight sections of racks"; the striking sunken niche displays for large-scale bottles; the lockers; the extended table tops.

For the economy-minded, Wine Cellar Innovations also carries a modular, put-it-together-yourself line. The redwood kit, with a useful 126-bottle lattice rack and a 48-bottle magnum rack, seems worthwhile, as does the country pine kit and its curved corner and individual-bottle racks.

Beautiful wood is part of the ambience of little West Cornwall, Connecticut, tucked away in lovely Litchfield County, in the northwestern corner of the state. For one thing, the town is the home of perhaps the most photogenic covered bridge in New England. The 242-foot red bridge, spanning the Housatonic River, was built in 1841 and has been in continuous service since 1864.

For another, it is also the home of New England Wine Cellars, which has built artful wooden cellars all over the United States, mostly in affluent suburbs of major cities. "We have also installed wine cellars in Europe," said Fred Tregaskis, the owner. "A very nice 6,000-bottle cellar in a wine and food store outside of Zurich comes to mind especially."

The ten years since the company's founding, in 1993, have shown steady growth, Tregaskis said. "We build 30 to 40 cellars a year, and employ three installation crews," he said. "Lately, our projects seem to entail more high-end presentation cellars and fewer utility-grade storage facilities.

"I haven't seen a great change in what customers request. Most clients have traveled to wine country in Europe and want to recreate their experiences there. They generally want an Old World look, a comfortable place to show, share and enjoy their wine collection.

"For one customer, we used black polished beach pebbles placed loose on the floor. This enabled him to be able to spit on the floor as in cellars he had been to in Burgundy. We use a lot of found objects, like carved stone sinks and old hardware from junk shops.

"I love to find old doors like the Art Deco stained doors used at The Breakers hotel in Palm Beach, Florida," Tregaskis went on. "A fly-fishing lodge in Montana gave us the caveat that no trees be cut for wood in its construction; the wine racks had to be built of recycled wood that we milled from railway trestles from Sonoma, California."

The way New England Wine Cellars works offers a glimpse into the way its competitors do.

"Clients now come mostly by way of referrals, or from work they may have seen at a wine store or at a restaurant," Tregaskis said. "They may have seen the spectacular cellar at The Breakers; at Atlas, a restaurant in Manhattan, or at 100 Market Street, in Portsmouth, New Hampshire.

"We schedule a meeting with them to determine their needs and budget. During that session, we listen to what kinds of wine they have or expect to have: How much is long-term storage? Are there large-format bottles? What is the architectural theme they want?

"We lay out a computer-aided-design drawing and proposal. Once we come to a design-and-price agreement, the customers are placed on the calendar and a start date is set. Often we work with the designer or architect on-site to keep a sense of continuity with the rest of the house."

Tregaskis found himself dissatisfied with refrigeration systems on the market. "Through-the-wall units were just too small and unreliable for our clients' expectations," he said. They were too noisy, producing vibration in cellars, and drying, causing corks to leak. His aim was both consistency of temperature, which he feels is "more vital than the 55 degree Fahrenheit temperature, the standard, and 50 percent to 70 percent relative humidity."

"Out of frustration, I worked with several refrigeration engineers to develop a climate-control air-ducted system, called CellarMate, that addresses the needs of a professional wine-cellar builder," Tregaskis said. "We market it internationally, and it accounts for about a third of our income."

The modular, or do-it-yourself kit, business is a strength of The *Wine Enthusiast* and *International Wine Accessories*, with both offering free assistance with wine cellar design. What does this mean? Read on.

Working With a Major Supplier

The *Wine Enthusiast*'s wine-storage consultants, based in the company's headquarters (which houses its showroom), in Elmsford, New York, in Westchester County, not far from Manhattan, provide advice on creating free-standing and custom cellars.

Callers are asked to describe their regional climate; the size of their actual or projected collection and future needs; their functional or decorative needs or both; and the sizes of the bottles in their holdings. They are asked to provide exactingly careful measurements of the spaces in their homes that would contain cellars, from a spare closet to a spare wing. (Since the *Enthusiast* cannot independently verify the measurements, it recommends a routine remeasurement and a sign-off by clients before construction of a cellar.)

First, potential clients fax a preliminary sketch showing the dimensions, the placement of doors, the size of the collection and type of racking sought. Then, the consultants, working by phone, e-mail and fax, develop a custom cellar design, which helps customers visualize their floor plans, and suggest a racking system that meets the customers' requirements. The consultants also propose other elements, including cooling units, choice of woods, flooring, moldings, decorative doors, etched-glass windows and artwork.

Finished designs are faxed to the potential client for approval, and, if the customer proceeds, the company puts together the system disassembled and ships it for installation. If a client wants an installer, the company will send one.

Often, buyers prefer to use local contractors or their own handymen.

The basic drawing is free; a client who wants more detailed renderings is charged $95 for a two-dimensional plan, $250 for a computer-aided three-dimensional plan and $395 for a full-color three-dimensional plan. The costs are deducted from the cellar price if the client gives the work a green light.

The *IWA* and *Enthusiast* catalogs show the elements of the put-it-together-yourself kits along with height, width and depth measurements, bottle-storage capacities, unit prices and shipping costs. (Incidentally, some professionals think nine-inch-deep racks are relatively unstable, and recommend 13-inch-deep racks for a better fit for your bottles.) The attraction for entry-level customers is undeniable, but consumers who are not handy or are impatient when faced with assembling furniture need to satisfy themselves first that they are not inviting frustration.

(You would be surprised at the number of freelance handymen and building superintendents who are asked to put together Ikea cabinets for tenants who are all thumbs; some handymen must explain to customers that electrical appliances, to run, must be plugged into the wall sockets.)

Beware of bins that must be put together with pegs that fit into holes; ultimately, the pegs come out. And be especially careful to avoid racks that must be affixed to walls; if you want them, make sure your walls can handle the attachment hardware. You do not want your family, especially if you have children, threatened by unstable or weakly held bins, especially in newly constructed buildings in which contractors may have, well, cut corners. When in doubt, be prudent; opt for free-standing units that need no external bracing.

In your planning, resist the inevitable impulse to stock the new cellar fully right away. Allot room for very long-term expansion based on calculations of how much wine you customarily use in a given time period and your projected

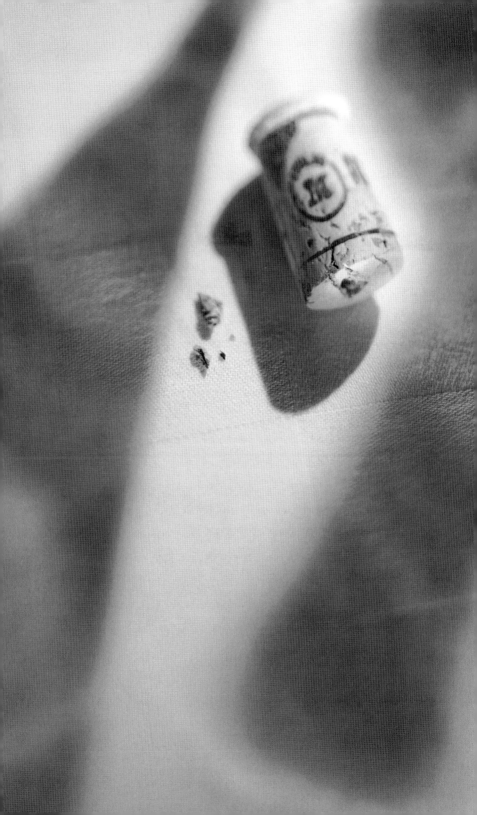

rate of growth of inventory in bottles for short-, medium- and long-term use.

Minimally, how much wine should you keep in your cellar? It depends on how many bottles you drink each week and the relative numbers of wines used from Monday through Friday (basic, friendly, good-tasting and not subject to searching aesthetic or critical analyses); on weekends (complex, interesting, a potpourri of subtleties); and on special occasions (great vintages, great producers, Chapter 11 bankruptcy prices).

Calculate your family's yearly consumption and multiply it by five. If you and your wife finish four bottles during the business week (vacation aside), that would come to 50 weeks multiplied by four, or 200 bottles a year: nearly 17 cases. Two wines each weekend would total 100 a year or nearly nine cases. Add perhaps 48 bottles of super-premiums throughout the year (some of them given as gifts): four cases. In all, you would consume, share and give away about 30 cases—a total of 360 bottles. Steady, systematic, astute buying, perhaps weekly, should keep the inventory at that level; you could also develop the habit of storing and inventorying a wine right after it arrives in the house.

The sizes most often found are half-bottles (375 milliliters); regular 750-milliliter bottles; liters; and magnums (the equivalent of two 750's, or 1.5 liters).

After that, you get into the so-called large-format sizes, all rare: the Marie-Jeanne (Bordeaux, 3 bottles in one, 2.25 liters); double magnum (Bordeaux) and Jeroboam (Burgundy, Champagne, 4 bottles in one, 3 liters) and Jeroboam (Bordeaux, 6 bottles in one, 4.5 liters); Rehoboam (Champagne, 6 bottles in one, 4.5 liters); Methuselah (Burgundy, Champagne, 8 in one, 6 liters); Imperial (Bordeaux, 8 bottles in one, 6 liters); Salamanazar (Champagne, 12 in one, 9 liters); Balthazar (Champagne, 16 in one, 12 liters); Nebuchadnezzar (Champagne, 20 in one, 15 liters); Melchior (Bordeaux, Champagne, 24 in one, 18 liters).

Incidentally, a case of magnums equals in content 12 standard bottles or nine liters. And, in the unlikely event that you bought a barrel of wine, it would contain 180 liters, or the equivalent of 240 standard bottles (20 cases). If you can't get the bung out, invite me over. I'll bring the wine thief—a long glass tube used to draw wine from barrels.

The Oxford Companion to Wine enlightens us thus: "The bottle has in its time been described as a suitable ration of wine for one person at a sitting, one person per day, and two people at a sitting." Well, ya pays yer money and ya takes yer cherce, as the hoary axiom goes.

And while we are focusing on bottles, one of the small entries in the *Oxford Companion* addresses an inescapable issue that bedevils even the most careful of collectors, bottle variation: "one of the more tantalizing aspects of wine appreciation."

"It is only to be expected with a product as sensitive to storage conditions as wine," the *Companion* goes on, "that bottles of the same wine will differ—perhaps because one has been exposed to higher temperatures or greater humidity. There can easily be a perceptible difference in quality and character between bottles from the very same case." Cork problems may contribute to such variations.

A Crucial Distinction

Cellars are passive or active (though one rarely encounters these contrasting terms). Passive cellars are naturally cool, moist chambers that require no intervention. The Platonic prototype would be the cool, moist, quiet caves of the Loire and Burgundy and Champagne regions. A rarity in the United States, they tend to be found in old country houses and on farm properties, and generations have used them to store food, as in root cellars.

In England, Scotland, Wales and Ireland and on the Continent passive cellars are also commonly visualized as creepy Charles Addams-like subterranean chateau chambers whose bins hold cobwebbed bottles with soiled labels that, indifferent to the rise and fall of national regimes, have slept undisturbed, even by resident ghosts, for decades, awaiting Prince Charming.

(I do not suggest that, like America's Robber Barons of the 19th century, you buy up whole castles, dismantle them for shipment and recreate them in an Indianapolis suburb. Built-in moisture is cheaper to arrange.)

Active cellars strive to reproduce the benefits conferred by passive cellars. They are created above or below ground, depend on air management and must have insulation on all four sides, as well as on the floor and on the ceiling, to maintain correct temperatures and humidity controls.

Wine is a supersensitive biochemical entity that, one sometimes thinks, could benefit from classical Freudian analysis. Famously, in the winery it suffers so-called bottle shock, from which it needs months to recover. It is traumatized by transoceanic transportation (especially when conditions turn mean in the North Atlantic), and even when shipped in temperature-controlled containers it needs time to find its identity (before that identity starts changing). Often it seems moody and introverted, and the full glass that seems outgoing and friendly at noon (like many business executives) comes across as grouchy and resistant at dinnertime (again, like many executives).

Although everything about your home may be friendly, its temperature, at 70 degrees or more during the cold season, is the foe of expensive wine that has been randomly stacked and stashed here and there, especially in closets and kitchens.

The physical enemies of cellared wine also include too much humidity or dampness, as well as light, vibration and inadequate ventilation. (Too often such deficiencies singly or collectively mistreat the stock in wine stores, not to speak of wholesalers' sprawling warehouses; consumers' only control is to select merchants carefully.)

In planning and building a cellar, if exquisite attention is not given to prospective threats to the well-being of one's wines, which become increasingly fragile as they age, the purposes of storage will be defeated. Bottles of still wine should be stored horizontally—in their original cases, in racks or in bins—to keep the corks moist (preventing shrinkage) and the air out. Air causes oxidation and accelerates the aging process.

With virtually no disagreement, the wine trade considers 55 degrees Fahrenheit (13 degrees Celsius) the perfect cellar temperature. The consensus on a workable constant-temperature range is 50 degrees Fahrenheit (10C) to 59 degrees Fahrenheit (15C); this span, experts believe, promotes steady, gradual maturation over a decade from the vintage date.

Cooler temperatures ranging, say, from 30 to 49 degrees Fahrenheit (from minus 1 degree Celsius to 9.4C) will slow the evolution. Under 30 degrees, the wine may freeze. (Wine freezes later than water because of its alcohol content.)

Conversely, temperatures from 60 to 72 degrees (16C to 22C) will hasten maturation, and any points above 72 will promote evaporation and deterioration.

Even as steady temperatures are crucial to the progressive evolution of wines, large and frequent swings are risky. Seasonal or annual drifts between 50 and 59 degrees Fahrenheit are not thought likely to compromise wine, but extreme, abrupt or too frequent spikes (like warming up during the day and cooling down at night) may play havoc with its complex chemistry. Such spikes can undo a fine wine if it goes from cellar to kitchen refrigerator and then, your mind changed, goes back to the cellar, only to return to the refrigerator again in a few days.

Do not—repeat not—store whites and sparkling wines in refrigerators for more than a week or so. This equipment is designed to chill food fast to prevent spoilage. It blasts cold air in order to create a suitable temperature, then turns off, and, when the temperature goes up again, blasts more cold air—a pattern that may be good for food but, when dryness and vibrations are added, undermines wine.

Stories are legion about wine being left too long in the sun and the heat of maritime and warehouse loading docks and being literally cooked to death; worse, the same thing has happened in distributors' (wholesalers) and retailers' warehouses, as the heat rises and envelops high-stacked palettes of wine.

In her splendid book *The Wine Bible* (Workman, 2001), Karen MacNeil writes: "According to research conducted at the Department of Viticulture and Enology at the University of California at Davis, the rate of chemical reactions in wine can double with each 18 degree Fahrenheit increase in temperature. Thus, a wine stored at 75 degrees Fahrenheit may change twice as fast as a wine stored at 57 degrees Fahrenheit" and, in the end, taste cooked. The expansions and contractions of wine in bottle caused by fluctuations of heat and cold can weaken and push out corks, causing "weeping," which is a form of leakage, and introducing hostile oxygen.

Humidity, like temperature, has make-or-break capabilities. Too little—a too-dry atmosphere—and corks will dry out, allowing oxidation. Too much humidity and, while dampness will not damage wine, it will cause mold, which destroys labels and undermines bottles' resale value in the auction market. (If corks turn moldy under their capsule, simply clean the cork with a damp paper towel before opening the bottle.) That is why every downstairs cellar must have an impermeable polyethylene barrier to block water vapor that wants to get in.

Informed opinion suggests that 60 percent to 70 percent relative humidity is ideal, that 75 percent is safe and that 80 percent should be the maximum allowable, but at that point it is getting dicey. Above 80 percent, you risk turning the labels and the wrong kind of wooden shelving into mold-sprouting jungles.

A simple hygrometer, which measures relative humidity in a cellar or cabinet, or a cellar gauge combining both a hygrometer and thermometer, can be found in hardware stores and at wine-specialty outlets, many of which have Internet addresses. If the cellar is large, more than one of each may be needed. (Do not confuse a hygrometer with a hydrometer, an instrument that measures the specific gravity of liquids.)

One digital noncable monitoring device, made by Oregon Scientific, uses remote sensors to track temperature and humidity in various parts of a cellar and transmit the data to a central monitor, which contains a memory that creates a record and sounds an alarm of the measurements get out of kilter. A smart, cheaper technique is to pass needle-based thermometers—the ones used for meat in ovens—through the corks of representative bottles centrally placed in bins.

Let There Be Little Light

Light and wine, even in tinted or dark bottles, are adversaries. (That's why you should never let a merchant give you a bottle out of his store window.) White wine in colorless glass is a sitting duck. Sunlight, which is good for grapes, heats up and thus subverts wine; so keep ultraviolet rays out of the cellar, and keep all cellar light, indirect or not, to the barest minimum. Better yet, keep the cellar dark except for your brief visits. As an added safety measure, let wine remain in its original wooden cases and boxes, though be watchful of floor dampness, which ruins cardboard.

Decorative candles, for fire reasons alone, should not share cellars with wood, no matter what décor fantasies the shelter magazines propagate; such photo shoots too often smack of hokum. By the same token (I appreciate that many collectors will find this advice disappointing), large-scale extended tastings, drinking, dining, music and conversation are out of place in a home cellar, even if restaurants promote such socializing in real or pseudo-cellars.

But all need not be lost. Space allowing, you, your family and your guests can relish the beauty of your collection through glass doors, possibly etched with a personal design, from a room adjacent to the cellar. (If you have bottomless pockets and a spacious wine cellar, you can create a dining room within the cellar that is sealed off from it on four sides by Thermopane glass.)

Richard M. Gold, Ph.D., a retired psychology professor at the University of Massachusetts at Amherst, is the author of *How and Why to Build a Wine Cellar*

(Sandhill Publishing, Post Office Box 9614, North Amherst, Massachusetts, 01059, third edition, 1996), which he describes, accurately, as an "underground classic."

"Twenty years ago," Gold said in an interview, "the controlling mood of the wine industry seemed to be to downplay" the issues of temperature and humidity in wine storage "lest it scare prospective customers away."

Then Robert M. Parker Jr., in what was his fledgling *Wine Advocate* newsletter, "began flogging the importance of proper shipping and storage," Gold said. "The result has been more fine-wine purchases and better storage. Proper home and industry storage conditions were not all that difficult, and, once achieved, liberated consumers from fear."

Gold's highly detailed book, laying out the nuts and bolts of building a passive cellar—one with no mechanical, only natural, refrigeration—has contributed significantly to that liberation.

"I couldn't interest a publisher or a bookstore chain, so I self-published it in 1983," he recalled. "After 19 years, 3 editions, and 11 printings, 38,000 copies have sold. It's running 2,000-plus every year, with no end in sight."

His book, stressing fundamentals in an agreeably sensible Trumanesque no-frills style, comes to mind here because he wants the lighting of a cellar kept basic. "I use a single 40-watt overhead fluorescent," he wrote. "When my fluorescent light was inadvertently left on overnight, the cellar temperature jumped 1 degree Fahrenheit (0.5C), demonstrating how even the heat from fluorescents can disturb cellar temperature." (Fluorescents, he says, are safer because they create less heat than incandescents.)

Gold is so careful he would not connect the light to an automatic timer. "It's likely to be relied on to turn the light off and then might fail," he said. "Better to feel that you have to turn it off manually. Also, if you set the auto timer when you enter for, say, 10 minutes, and then linger, it's likely to shut off when you have the Lafite in your hand. Very dangerous."

If there is a limit to human patience with the mercurial, virtually neurotic nature of wine, it will surely crack when told that stored wine is potentially sensitive to, and vulnerable to, vibration. Although science thinks this is the case, it does not yet have proof. Anecdotal evidence of a threat is so voluminous that danger from vibration should be treated as if it were gospel. It is plausible to believe that disturbances will dislodge accumulated sediment, thus influencing wine chemistry in important bottles nearing their prime. Street vibrations from traffic and in metropolitan areas from subways, along with apartment house disturbances like elevators' movements, can upset wine chemistry's repose as surely as can appliances like washing machines and dryers, and mechanisms like furnaces and water heaters (here we are also talking about lethal heat).

Wine's bottomless vulnerability extends to off-odors. No offensive smells from household-cleaning products, chemicals, paint, detergents, perfumed sprays, perishable foods, garbage, dirt, pools of rank water and from outside should be allowed in the cellar atmosphere. They may well seep through the cork into the wine. If these aromas threaten or are present, aerate the cellar by venting; electronic air cleaners offer another option.

If your wine is stored not in a basement but in your apartment or house, the same do's and don'ts that apply downstairs apply upstairs. In the kitchen? Fuhgeddaboutit. If you absolutely must stock the kitchen in the predictable way that home-design gurus always recommend—under the marble-topped, two-sink central island or a counter (or bar in another room)—then limit the display to a couple of dozen bottles for short-term drinking. Luxury wines will be done in by the menacing combination of temperature oscillations, invasive sunlight and artificial light, and dishwasher and refrigerator vibrations.

If common sense points, as usual, to a closet in a quiet area, make sure no heat comes from floor or other pipes in or near it; since heat rises, keep the bottles near the floor and off shelves. Avoid exterior walls, which absorb and radiate heat. Do not even think, for one microsecond, of going near the attic: the ultimate no-no. Especially avoid garage storage; it can be too iffy, and you do not want to open a case of rare Burgundy only to find yourself in the vinegar business.

Free-standing temperature- and humidity-controlled wine cellars that fit into wooden cabinets and double as custom-made furniture, with wooden or glass doors and locks and keys, are less expensive than a cellar created from the ground up, especially for small collections. Sometimes these devices are loosely called wine coolers. (Do not confuse the metal versions with refrigerators, which some resemble.)

Many ready-to-use cellars sheathed in credenzas, armoires, breakfronts and cabinets with wood finishes like natural through dark oak, cherry, maple, walnut and mahogany, and with variously patterned doors, are especially handsome and would fit beautifully into rooms featured in, say, *Architectural Digest*.

These basic-through-luxury cellars combining fixed and sliding shelves, with interior lights that can be kept on or off, are plugged into standard household outlets upon delivery and immediately are up and running. They can be placed to show off your collection, or, more modestly, can fit into remote corners, niches and in closets. The storage capabilities, varying with brands and styles, run approximately from 16 bottles to 1,000, including standard and large-format sizes. (The glass in doors tends to be tinted, sometimes double paned, in order to neutralize ultraviolet light, which can penetrate even green glass bottles.)

Rigorous comparison-shopping is indispensable, as these devices are major items in catalogs like *International Wine Accessories*, *Wine Enthusiast* and the *Wine Appreciation Guild*. Check out such brands as Avanti, BreezAire, Chambrair, ChateauCraft, EuroCave, Franklin, Haier, Koolspace, Le Cache, Le Cellier, Marvel, Sub-Zero, Transtherm, U-Line, Vinocave, Vinocraft, Vino-thèque, Vinotemp and Vintage Keeper.

At their best, electrified wine cabinets attempt to replicate the conditions of traditional underground wine cellars: humidity, constant temperature, natural ventilation, darkness, freedom from vibration.

All consultations of catalogs from distributors of luxury merchandise like wine-storage cabinets should be supplemented by patient exploration of the producers' Web sites, which may yield a deeper understanding of the products under consideration. You may also encounter products not advertised in print by distributors.

Certain units are so sophisticated that they have multiple compartments with multiple temperature zones. Chambrair, a British company, has advertised a model with six separate zones, descending in degrees of chill, for older and aged red wines; younger or full-bodied reds; mature, full-bodied whites and light reds; elegant dry whites; rosé and medium to sweet wines; and sparkling and dessert wines.

Red wines intended for near-term consumption should be stored at 55 to 65 degrees Fahrenheit (13 Celsius to 18C); dry whites, at 49 to 56 degrees Fahrenheit (9.4C to 13C); rosés, from 49 to 51 Fahrenheit (9.4C to 10.6C); and sparkling wines, 45 to 49 degrees Fahrenheit (7C to 9.4C).

Since bottle shapes vary, you must inquire into storage capabilities for Alsace and German wines (consider the slim Mosel style and the small Franconian bocksbeutel), for half-bottles and large-scale bottles like magnums and Jeroboams.

The Wine Appreciation Guild (www.wineappreciation.com), in San Francisco, which has merchandised wine accessories since 1973, is perhaps best known for its in-depth offerings of books. Its mailings are always worth scanning, if only to catch up with a worthy new book that may have escaped attention in annual year-end pre-Christmas roundups in the general media. The Guild, both a publisher and a distributor, maintains a large-scale backlist that can tempt bookish novices and connoisseurs alike.

The Guild imports and markets a wine-cellar line that, on its face at least, seems worth looking into. (I have had no experience with it.) Called Silent Cellar, it is made by the Domestic division of Electrolux, the Swedish appliance giant. "This is the only home wine cellar that has no motor, no compressor and is totally free of vibration and noise," says Elliott Mackey, the Guild's vice president of marketing. "It utilizes a technology called absorption refrigeration, which has no moving parts, a long life and energy efficiency, and was developed for hotel mini-bars and hospital refrigerators."

Other wine cellars use a so-called cold wall system for cooling, Mackey said. Cabinet temperature is controlled gently by moving refrigerant though the interior walls and recycling humidity. "However, these cellars use an electric motor and compressor, which cycles on and off to maintain the temperature. Although barely detectable, the subtle noise and vibrations over many years may harm the long-term aging of wine," he said. Silent Cellars models offer varying bottle capacities. They may attract collectors whose wines need aging for 10 years or more.

A useful though pricey alternative is the totally insulated prefabricated-wood walk-in wine cellar—in effect, a room within a room—that can contain thousands of bottles. It may take a workman or two a day to put it together, including the lighting, ceiling, walls, floor, door, wine and case racks and cooling system. If you move, it can be dismantled and then reconstituted in your new residence.

Air-conditioning can be no less dangerous to wine. While cooling a room, air-conditioners dry out the air. Generally, they are not designed to perform properly in the 55 to 58 degree Fahrenheit and 55 percent to 75 percent humidity range. You must buy units designed specifically for wine cellars if you want to maintain the proper environment.

When the temperature rises, the bottle expands, but the wine expands seven times more than the glass. The pressure created forces wine out of the bottle. As the bottle cools down, a vacuum is created, sucking oxygen-rich air through or around the cork and into the bottle. The oxygen finds its way to the air space, called ullage, that was created between the top of the wine and bottom of the cork during filling and that moved elsewhere when the bottle was stored on its side. A certain quantity of ullage is indispensable; otherwise, minor changes in temperature might push wine out of the bottle, causing shifts and weaknesses in the cork's grip.

In a mature wine, sizeable ullage—at the base of the neck or below—must be interpreted as a warning of oxidation. Auction houses' catalogs routinely contain graphics of Bordeaux and Burgundy bottles that depict ullage levels, which then turn up in descriptions of the lots: for example, NYWines/Christie's, in detailing six bottles of 1967 Château Guiraud, a Sauternes, reported: "Levels: five bottom neck or better, one top shoulder."

A Small History Lesson

Since *The Wine Enthusiast* has been in the forefront of wine cellar merchandising nationwide, I asked Adam M. Strum, the chairman and chief executive officer of its catalog house and publisher and editor of its magazine, to provide his perspective on the small history of the market.

His reply: "Today, sales of wine cellars and wine coolers have proliferated much as VCR and microwave sales did in the 1980s and the personal computer and cell phone did in the 1990s.

"While wine cellars are still not available in most general appliance stores, wine coolers are sold in Walmart and most such stores. Coolers are small refrigerator-type products with wine racks; they provide constant temperature but do not supply the humidity control that cellars provide.

"It is astonishing that cellars and coolers, which were so esoteric and deemed important only by the very affluent and most ardent wine lovers 15 years ago, would have grown into a mainstream business. This trend has steadily paralleled the increase in wine consumption and the growth in wealth.

"Early *Enthusiast* catalogs (1980-85) devoted only four pages to cellars (there were no coolers then). Today, the catalog devotes more than 20 pages to cellaring.

"There were two distinct ways to maintain wines in the early days. First, there was the pre-built, free-standing cellars dominated by a unique cellar called Vinothèque. This large wooden box held some 360 bottles of wine in individual pressed-wood racks. At the top was a small unit that provided a convection cooling system that kept the temperature at about 55 degrees. Second, there were providers of custom redwood racking who would create racking for any space—a closet, basement—coupled with a cooling unit properly sized for the space and the correct insulation. This amounted to a walk-in cellar.

"*Wine Enthusiast* was the first company to market these products nationally, and they sold fairly well. During this period, our first million catalogs were mailed, perhaps helping subliminally to introduce wine cellaring to Americans. We created a staff of consultants who were trained to be storage authorities. But supply barely met demand at this time, and there were waits up to three months for the delivery of a Vinothèque and of racking and cooling.

"The 1982 Bordeaux vintage, highly touted by the critic Robert M. Parker Jr., created a huge demand for cellaring when the wine began being delivered in 1985. *Wine Enthusiast* formed a partnership with EuroCave, a large French wine-cellar factory, to help fill this demand and began importing them. EuroCaves were different from Vinothèques in that they were not made of wood but were aluminum and laminated. EuroCave's reliability combined with French panache and styling enabled it to dominate the cellar business from 1985 to 1992.

"The sale of cellars entered the mainstream in the 1990s as the sales of red wine exploded following the so-called French Paradox segment of '60 Minutes,' which touted the benefits of moderate consumption in 1991.

"During the 1990s, *Wine Enthusiast* carried a small wine Sanyo cooler that held 24 bottles of wine and sold quite well. In the late 1990s, we developed a 34-bottle and later a 50-bottle cellar in the same style, both made in Asia. These appliances provided a ready-access cooler to augment large cellars, an affordable free-standing cooler for small collections and a cooler that was front-vented and could be integrated into a kitchen. These coolers sold for $299, $399 and $599, respectively, and could be delivered for under $100 anywhere in the nation.

"Suddenly there were entry-level wine coolers for the beginner, and, even as we embraced this idea so did competitive refrigerator manufacturers such as Sub-Zero, Viking, U-Line and others. The marketplace is currently glutted with low-end entry-level coolers just as the consumer is experiencing the benefits of a glut of wine!

"There are so many choices for storage that growth of the field has been extraordinary. What was a $25 million business in 1990, in which *Wine Enthusiast* enjoyed at least 65 percent of the market, has grown to as much as a $250 million dollar business, in which we have about a 30 percent market share.

"To demonstrate the growth of the market: In 1985, the first year we sold a significant amount of wine cellars, revenue from cellar sales came to $10 million. The next major leap was in 1992, with $30 million in sales; then in 2000 with $50 million, and in 2002 with $60 million."

Organizing Your Cellar

Every cellar needs an organizing principle. The right software—the contemporary version of the traditional cellar book—enables you to tailor the computerized management of your cellar storage bins to your needs. Not insignificantly, a list of your holdings is a typical necessity in insurance policies. The basic idea is that you should be able to learn in a flash what you own, where it is and what the stock levels are. The system, of course, implies personal discipline: you have to allow time to adjust the records every time you add to or subtract from the cellar.

How to organize the wine in a database? Let us count the ways:

By category of wine (still wines against this wall, Champagne against the far wall); by color (red here, white over there); by country or by region or appellation (United States, California, Sonoma County, Green Valley); by grape; by producer or estate; by wine name; by vineyard name; by vintage year; by price paid (per bottle and/or case) and current value as the wine appreciates or declines; by the date and the source of the acquisition (name of retailer, producer, auction house, gift-giver or locale when you were on vacation); alphabetically; by numerical and other ratings, your own and from wine publications and critics; by the possible maturation time line (fairly difficult to guess); by bottle sizes, from half-bottles through the largest of the large-format bottles; by bins assigned to wooden cases; by taste characteristics and progressions from dryness through sweetness; by food-matching criteria; by wines for weekdays and for weekends; for trial drinking ("must be done this week, before the retailer's nonreplenishable supply runs out"); for special occasions; by a separation of his and hers. You name it.

Joshua Wesson, co-founder and co-chief executive officer of Best Cellars, a customer-friendly chain that sells most wines at $15 or less (in New York City, Seattle, Dallas, Washington D.C., Boston and Brookline, Massachusetts), thinks a private cellar should replicate the way the stores' stock is arranged. As he puts it: "Though there are many sensible ways to lay out a cellar, none is as useful as an organizational scheme based upon taste. This is especially true if the rack you're filling happens to be your first, for it's a primary axiom of collecting that it's far harder to drink up a cellar than to assemble one.

"If you opt for a traditional ordering scheme, you'll have no problem placing your bottles in some sort of stately progression from Amador to Zell, or aligoté to zinfandel. But the next time you open your cellar door to grab a perfect partner for your pepperoni pizza, your layout won't help you a whit.

"Precisely because most of us know what tastes we like in wine and, more importantly, what tastes we don't like, using taste or wine style as an organizational guide is an instantly attractive and intuitively simple method for classifying and arranging any wine you own.

"At Best Cellars, we use eight taste categories for our wines: fizzy, fresh, soft, luscious, juicy, smooth, big and sweet. You might select a greater or lesser number of categories for your cellar. Whatever set you settle upon, if you use taste as an organizing principle, you'll find yourself facing only one real problem: how best to fill all those missing holes in your favorite cave."

There might be, too, a sop to serendipity. As a teenager I discovered the delight of finding an overlooked $1 or $5 bill in a pocket. A lifelong game ensued: I periodically plant a $10 bill in an old jacket, and years later "discover" it, with delight. This led to another game: I store good, age-worthy bottles outside their regular zones in my racks, and later "serendipitously" find them, and am invariably rewarded when they're opened. The downside, of course, is that if you don't "discover" them in good time, they may have faded.

The Way It Is, Mostly

When you read about wine cellars in glossy magazines, you may think the owners, usually portrayed as high rollers, are in heaven, and, in some cases, they are (figuratively). But keep in mind that life's usual appearance vs. reality duality are present, and the stories you read do not necessarily dig into the way most serious wine lovers live their wine cellar experiences. The big-bucks wine cellars in picture-perfect too-good-to-be-true houses, of the pristine sort exalted in, say, *Architectural Digest*, are relatively few and far between.

Take the experience of Lisa Shara Hall. I first meet Lisa at the International Pinot Noir Celebration in the Willamette Valley, in Oregon, in 2000. I was immediately impressed by her no-nonsense, refuse-to-be-glitzed attitude toward wine. She is the senior editor of *Wine Business Monthly* and winebusiness.com, author of *The Wines of the Pacific Northwest* (Mitchell Beazley) and lives in Portland, Oregon.

Here's how she responded to my request to tell her cellar story:

"My husband, Kirk, and I have a wine cellar that is not ideal. We never sat down and made a plan or took the time to properly design something that could meet our needs over time.

"When we bought our house, we totally gutted it. We used our architect friend Ernie Munch, who had also designed Domaine Drouhin Oregon by then, but not yet WillaKenzie Estate or Domaine Serene, in the Willamette Valley.

"We had a modest wine collection when we remodeled in 1993, perhaps 500 bottles, as I had begun to write about wine and was developing more than a casual or social interest in the subject.

"I don't think we ever planned to 'collect' wines, just store them for later enjoyment. We still don't collect per se, but we don't want to miss out on terrific wines from terrific vintages, and we keep buying.

"We keep lists, but it is a burden at times trying to decide what to drink. As with any large wine list, it can be very hard to choose—or, in our case, to find the bottle.

"We asked Ernie to design a built-in underground cabinet that could accommodate our collection and stay cool. Our usable basement space is limited. Heating ductwork snakes through all rooms in the basement, lowering the ceiling and making anything built-in difficult.

"Ernie designed a beautiful wine storage unit: a built-in cabinet that fitted, in our basement, into underground contours beneath a bay window in the room above. Temperature is controlled pretty naturally; the room is not heated, and the basement keeps cool all year round—about 65 degrees, without dramatic fluctuations. Behind two thick (insulated) clear fir double doors (locked with French door and window locks that are Ernie's signature window closure) stand three columns of drawers, each drawer on easy sliders, each outfitted for six individually cradled bottles. There are 33 drawers total. Around the doors—above, on the sides, are 12 open bins suitable for magnums—our favorite party size; for those long-necked bottles that don't fit in the drawers (sadly we didn't anticipate that); and just more storage.

"Total capacity is about 350 bottles, and when we built the unit, we thought that was ample forever, as we also had a small storage unit in use. But as our palates grew, our wine buying grew. And as we discovered new regions and wines, we bought them, too. A wine professional's palate and buying habits evolve the same way anybody else's does.

"But we outgrew our storage in two years. Although the cabinet is still in use, we have resorted to serial EuroCave purchases. Our bottle collection grew quickly, from those first 500 bottles or so to about 3,200 currently (and growing!).

We have different wines allocated to different cave spaces now, as we have been too lazy and cheap to bite the bullet and convert the whole room to a temperature-controlled, shelf-lined wine cellar.

"Tuscan, Amarone, Champagne and Rhône wines and all large-format bottles live in the original built-in unit. Bordeaux and Burgundy go in one plug-in unit. Chablis, riesling, grüner veltiner, Barolo and Barbaresco are in another plug-in unit. Spanish wines hide in an armoire with angled shelves that my brother-in-law converted for us as our wedding present.

"Oregon and Washington wines—purchased primarily for a library for my work—plus many new purchases from all over are parked in the same room as the classy Ernie-built cabinet but without any additional insulation or cooling. We need even more controlled space that we've got now. The Ernie-designed cabinet will stay unchanged and in use no matter what we ultimately wind up doing, which better be soon, as the cases are stacking up.

"Alas, the cabinet has not been a weather-perfect system. During particularly heavy rains with wind, water saturates the earth, and, as the basement level is sited slightly downhill, water occasionally comes in under the earth-hugging unit, not harming bottles in the cabinet but causing all kinds of problems for the boxes of bottles that are stacked on the floor of the same room. We have since placed wooden pallets on the floor and stacked cases on those. Not ideal.

"Both my husband and I both are wine professionals. Kirk is corporate counsel for the Northwest's largest distributor. He has a finely developed and sophisticated palate, and while we love many of the same wines, he doesn't share all of my passion for Northwest wines, which of course are an occupational necessity for me. As professionals you would think we have the bottle storage problem licked.

"Nope. Think again."

The Best
and the Biggest

The high-powered Ursula Hermacinski, who shares Zachys' auctioneering duties with the witty, cherubic Fritz Hatton, argues persuasively for acquiring large-format bottles, the so-called kings of the auction. Writing in the catalog for the house's second sale, in December 2002, she explained that interest in these terms: "ageability, investment opportunity, rarity and sociability."

Wines tend to mature more slowly and subtly in large-size bottles than in smaller bottles because, it is thought, the proportion of oxygen to liquid volume is smaller in them.

Collectors, Ms. Hermacinski wrote, "find value in the comfort of knowing that large-format bottles can stand up to a cellar slumber decades long." They draw huge prices. For example, at an Sotheby's/Aulden Cellars auction in December 2002 an exceptionally rare Methuselah of 1989 Romanée-Conti from the Domaine de la Romanée-Conti, estimated at $18,000 to $25,000, fetched $23,500 (including the buyer's premium). A double magnum of 1992 Screaming Eagle cabernet sauvignon, a Napa Valley cult wine estimated at $6,500 to $8,500, realized $9,106.

As for socializing, imagine the glow felt by generous hosts and valued guests when a magnum, Marie-Jeanne or double magnum is hauled from its cradle, dusted off, opened and poured—hospitality that quietly announces that an expensive treasure is being shared. Who would forget the moment? In affluent homes and certain high-style restaurants, it is fascinating to watch a gleaming giant bottle being decanted and poured while gripped by a specially designed brass cradle resembling a Napoleonic artillery piece; when hand-cranked, the mechanism tilts the bottle, with a ceremonial slowness, from a near-vertical to a horizontal position.

A Cellar
Away From Home

If your living circumstances prevent you from having a weighty, diversified cellar at home, cellars in warehouses or in merchants' storage facilities may provide an alternative, but they obliterate spontaneity and limit your freedom of action. Generally, appointments have to be made to pick up wine. If your merchant offers no-cost warehousing, ask how long it would last, how the wine is insured and what the fees would be afterward. At best, outside bins should be seen as temporary solutions. If you must rent a commercial warehouse's lockers, inquire outside the warehouse about its reliability and inside about its liability: too many people in too many cities have been burned by theft.

Whether your cellar is ensconced in your home or outside, it must be carefully insured. It's likely that a minor collection may fall under your homeowner's policy, but only for theft, fire and a disaster like flooding, not for accidental breakage, which accounts for considerable loss.

Internet visits to organizations that store wine for outsiders should provide a round picture of general practices, charges and possible problems, even if the warehouses are far from where you live.

In New York City, Acker Merrall & Condit, an Upper West Side merchant and auction house, advertises its storage facility and its terms on www.ackerwines.com. Another model might be Zachys, which is a large wine shop in Scarsdale, New York, in suburban Westchester County, and also has an auction arm (www.zachys.com); make a point of reading the insurance options it offers.

Patrick W. Fegan, director of the Chicago Wine School, recommends the Strongbox Wine Cellar (www.winestorage.com, two locations) and the East Bank Wine Storage (www.eastbankwine.com, two locations) in his hometown.

In the San Francisco Bay area, check out Marin Wine Vaults in San Rafael, California (www.marinwinevaults.com). If you visited the office of Marin Wine Vaults to ask about a lease and insurance, Dawn Solon, the manager, would recommend that if you had homeowner's or renter's insurance you ought to check with your agent. "Some policies do offer off-site storage coverage," she said. "However, wine is considered high-risk since it is perishable," so you may need to add a rider on your current policy.

I asked Ms. Solon to explain the company's security measures further. "We provide excellent cooling and humidity control and have the maintenance done on the system every three months," she said. "We provide a backup generator in case of power loss. We have an incredible security system: each vault is individually alarmed, and each vault was built with one-way screws. Every time someone puts in their security code or opens or shuts their door, it shows on my security monitor, a voice tells me and it prints out. If someone should cut the tenant's lock and open the door, an alarm would go off, it would appear on my monitor. If someone cut an alarm wire, there would be an alarm, and the location would show up on my monitor.

"If a pipe broke and there was water damage, we are not responsible. If a pipe leaked and we did not fix it, we would be responsible.

"When I present our lease to a prospective tenant, I inform them: 'This is a typical lease. Ninety-seven percent of it is saying we are not responsible.' This is a pretty standard business practice. Look at any lease you sign. We have done everything we can to protect the tenant's wine, and as a business we also need to protect ourselves."

Marin provides potential customers with a fine-wine insurance brochure put out by the Insurance Corporation of Hannover, which lists the name of an agent, Thomson & Pratt Insurance Associates, in Santa Monica, California, which will provide them with wine insurance.

The Chubb Group of Insurance Companies has long been identified with speciality insurance, including wine collectors' insurance. "Typically, homeowners insurance alone does not address your needs as a wine collector," the organization says. Its all-risk coverage for fire, theft and breakage merits investigation. Its Web site (www.chubb.com) lists options: "For one or more bottles valued at less than $10,000 each, you can purchase 'blanket' coverage under one lump sum. More expensive items can be specifically listed on the policy, with each bottle described and individually insured (itemized coverage) for a specific value."

The issues you want to look into with any potential insurer include availability of coverage in your home state (it might not exist), appraisals, personal record-maintenance (here's where your database and computer earn their keep), deductibles, worldwide coverage (is my collection covered both at home here in Skokie, a Chicago suburb, and in my country house on the Upper Peninsula of Michigan?), coverage of recently purchased wine, and payment of the replacement cost rather than the original cost.

Furnishing a Cellar

Whether your cellar occupies a corner or a chamber, the decorative arts should play a role. From time immemorial, artists of all kinds—painters, sculptors, woodworkers, metalworkers, glassmakers, you name it—have turned to vineyard and drinking imagery and themes for inspiration. The richness of it all—the thrill of it all, really—came back when a newly arrived catalog offered (for $350, it's not cheap) a beautiful tapestry reproducing a famous 15th-century one in the Musée de Cluny, the great Paris museum, that depicts winemaking in the Middle Ages.

I would like to hang it, I thought, in the same room with my beloved reproduction of a Lewis Comfort Tiffany stained-glass window depicting a grape arbor, bought from the Metropolitan Museum of Art in New York years ago.

While vigilantly avoiding the world of encumbering, virtually useless wine tchotchkes, beware of the kitschy, maudlin, even embarrassing paintings of vineyard scenes hawked by the wine industry. Too many look like failed bucolic Hollywood props for 1940's Technicolor boy-meets-girl cavortings.

You can find exuberant artworks by the popular painter and illustrator Wayne Ensrud, whose endearing and witty representations of Parisian cafes like Les Deux Magots, La Closerie des Lilas and Brasserie Lipp have graced summertime Sherry-Lehmann catalogs on and off for years. His studio is in Manhattan; his work, influenced by his mentor Oskar Kokoschka, can be found on the Web; he is well known for posters of fancifully rendered Bordeaux chateaus.

Mounted or framed vineyard maps, especially those from Editions Benoit, in Paris, are decorative and informational. I am especially fond of a striking two-map set showing the Côte d'Or in Burgundy. One covers the Côte de Beaune, the other the Côte de Nuits; both are about six feet tall and two feet wide, and are sold by the Burgundy Wine Company, a Manhattan wine merchant. These detailed maps, by Sylvain Pitiot and Pierre Poupon, show every vineyard in the region, its name, classification and topography. Frequently consulted, they help make sense of Burgundy, which is not easy.

You Could Look It Up

Minimally, a cellar library should include such basic, indispensable portable annuals as *Hugh Johnson's Pocket Wine Book* (Mitchell Beazley) and *Oz Clarke's Pocket Wine Guide* (Harcourt). Buy them in November or December, when next year's edition reaches stores, as a guide to holiday shopping. (Both fit purses and briefcases more readily than pockets.) Both are the ultimate desert-island manuals. (I keep two sets—one at my *New York Times* desk, the other in my home office—and routinely consult them every day.)

A-list reference works must include:

Oz Clarke's New Wine Atlas (Harcourt, 2002; new edition, fully revised and updated, with extraordinary, standard-setting multidimensional maps);

The World Atlas of Wine, by Hugh Johnson and Jancis Robinson (Mitchell Beazley, 2001; fifth edition, completely revised);

The Oxford Companion to Wine, edited by Jancis Robinson (Oxford University Press, 1999; second edition);

Oz Clarke's Encyclopedia of Grapes, by Clarke and Margaret Rand (Harcourt, 2001);

Michael Broadbent's Vintage Wine: Fifty Years of Tasting, Three Centuries of Wine (Harcourt, 2002);

The Taste of Wine: The Art and Science of Wine Appreciation, by Emile Peynaud (translated by Michael Schuster; Wine Appreciation Guild, 1987);

Parker's Wine Buyer's Guide, by Robert M. Parker Jr., with Pierre-Antoine Rovani (A Fireside Book, published by Simon & Schuster; paperback, sixth edition, 2002);

The Vintner's Art: How Great Wines Are Made, by Hugh Johnson and James Halliday (Simon & Schuster, 1992);

Terroir: The Role of Geology, Climate, and Culture in the Making of French Wines, by James E. Wilson (Mitchell Beazley, 1998);

Côte d'Or: A Celebration of the Great Wines of Burgundy, by Clive Coates (University of California Press, 1997);

B-list reference works such as:

Wine for Dummies, by Ed McCarthy and Mary Ewing-Mulligan (IDG Books Worldwide, paperback, second edition, 1998; watch for a third edition);

Windows on the World Complete Wine Course: 2003, by Kevin Zraly (Sterling), revised annually;

Champagne for Dummies, by Ed McCarthy (IDG Books Worldwide, paperback, 1999);

The Wine Bible, by Karen MacNeil (Workman Publishing, paperback, 2001);

Understanding Wine Technology: A Book for the Nonscientist That Explains the Science of Winemaking, by David Bird (The Wine Appreciation Guild, paperback, 2002);

American Vintage: The Rise of American Wine, by Paul Lukacs (Houghton Mifflin, 2000);

And such current books as:

Vino Italiano: The Regional Wines of Italy, by Joseph Bastianich and David Lynch (Clarkson Potter, 2002);

The Wine Avenger, by Willie Gluckstern (A Fireside Book, published by Simon & Schuster, paperback, 1998);

The Pleasures of Wine: Selected Essays, by Gerald Asher (Chronicle Books, 2002);

Here are indispensable publications and Internet sites:

Decanter magazine, London, and www.decanter.com (I write for both*)*;

The Wine News and www.thewinenews.com (I write for both);

The Wine Advocate and RobertParker.com;

International Wine Cellar and www.internationalwinecellar.com;

Wine and Spirits and wwwwineandspiritsmagazine.com;

Wine Spectator and www.winespectator.com;

Wine Enthusiast and www.winemag.com.

Paraphernalia or Tchotchkes?

One person's apparatus is another's tchotchke. Especially in furnishing a cellar. The storage space can resemble the spare, understated beauty of a Shaker kitchen—clean right down to its bones—or Aunt Flo's Knickknackerie on the boardwalk of a heavily touristed seaside resort. I keep frequently used gadgets, all inexpensive, to the barest minimum.

I am fond of an Anderson Valley Winegrowers Association's plastic-covered place mat that on both sides is chockablock with information about this wonderful cool-climate terrain in Mendocino County, California, just north of Napa and Sonoma. I picked it up at a vertical tasting in Manhattan sponsored by Milla Handley of Handley Cellars, and use it to protect from staining the butcher-block kitchen counter on which I do all my tastings. The association (www.avwines.com) can explain how to obtain it.

Though the choice of a corkscrew may seem like a trifling matter, it is not. The hedonist's relationship to every facet of wine life requires total pleasure—total grace—in every act, especially the central ritual of opening a bottle.

If you have ever closely watched a baseball player's yes and no movements while selecting a bat to do his bidding when dealing with the fundamentally adverse conditions of home plate, you can appreciate why, similarly, a corkscrew must appeal to one's psychology and physical needs. The commonplace practice of plugging a rudimentary T-shaped corkscrew into a bottle and then putting the bottle between your legs and using main force to withdraw the cork is Neanderthal.

My favorite is a solidly made stainless-steel corkscrew known universally as the waiter's friend, a kind of kid brother of the Swiss Army knife, backed up by the Screwpull for use when a cork is stubborn. Many in winedom consider the Screwpull a godsend—child's play to operate—and while I own one, and more-complicated apparatus as well, it is less gratifying than a rudimentary waiter's corkscrew: Maybe opening wine with the offhand deftness of an apron-wearing waiter in an outdoor café in Lyon makes me feel, well, appreciated.

The Screwpull, invented by an industrial engineer in 1979, comes in both a pricey lever model and a simpler table model, the latter resembling a clothespin whose legs surround a long Teflon-coated helix. The device is placed vertically over a cork and the top of the bottle's neck, its handle is turned and, presto, out slides the cork. For picnics, use Screwpull's pocket model.

For years, I prized and used almost exclusively the now nearly vanished Ah-So, a small opener with two flat flexible metal prongs issuing from the base of an oval handle that resembles a Japanese ideogram. (Actually, it was patented in America in the late 1800's.) The prongs were slipped between the cork and both sides of a bottle's mouth, the device was rocked gently back and forth until its handle sat on top of the cork, and then the cork was slowly twisted out, leaving no damage and only slight indentions, if any, on the sides. The Ah-So's grip is indispensable on older Bordeaux, whose corks tend to weaken from saturation and age. After a long prong broke when wedged between a hard, unyielding artificial noncork stopper and the glass, the Ah-So was not replaced, though ultimately it will be.

Its successor was a simple fold-up waiter's corkscrew, which can be carried in pocket or purse, given to me by a Portuguese producers' consortium. I loved its curved, seemingly soft and comfortable body, which contrasted with sharp-edged metal in other versions that, when pressure was applied, creased and hurt my right-hand fingers or the whole hand. The sharply pointed spiral (an auger or helix, called a worm), which I screwed into the cork just off-center, was long and compact; this feature created a firm grip in the cork, enabling it to be eased out with minimal pressure. The most efficient auger is a spiral that winds around an imaginary cylinder. The least efficient is a spiral that winds around a central metal shank.

After my overworked waiter's corkscrew broke and its soul flew to Sommeliers' Heaven, its successor was, briefly, the winged corkscrew sold in every supermarket: the kind whose two handles seem in flight as the helix bites into a cork. Its thick shank too often penetrated past the bottom of corks, leaving, when the wine was recorked and refrigerated or left on the dining-room table, a hole through which oxygen passed, hastening oxidation or dulling the wine. Though smooth, its shank chewed up the cork, unpleasantly sprinkling brown pieces on the table or on the wine. Whenever that happens, I feel like a doofus. (The mid-priced Pedro lever corkscrew, with wings, made by Monopol, a German company, frequently gets high marks.)

A corkscrew with an extra-long worm may be needed if your wine collection is heavy in Bordeaux and Italian wines that use extra-long corks; additionally, a long worm is handy when a cork breaks during extraction and its parts need separate retrieval. Make sure the corkscrew's small foldout knife blade is serrated and sharp, the better to cut dense foil enclosing the cork just beneath the flange near the mouth.

As a purist, I do not own the waiter's corkscrew with, at one end, a cap opener for bottled water, beer and soda. But, happily, I do possess an all-metal ergonomic Chateau Laguiole, from France, perhaps the world's finest corkscrew producer. Somehow, it does not make me aspire to handmade Laguioles that come with handles of olive wood, juniper wood, rosewood or cow horn, each stored in a leather pouch.

If a chunk of cork drops into the bottle, the sky will not fall. Have at hand an inexpensive cork retriever, found readily at bar-supply houses; it consists of at least three long wire rods with hooks at the bottom that can surround and grasp cork, which is then hauled through the neck and mouth.

Among other necessary accessories are a foil cutter; a DropStop, a thin, foldable, washable disk that fits tightly into a bottle's mouth and prevents drips that stain the tablecloth during pouring; a tapered bottle stopper, although the

original cork, if cleanly removed and wiped free of any mold on top, suffices; and a simple nickel-plated Champagne sealer that keeps the fizz airtight—perhaps one your favorite restaurant uses (the most reliable versions have clamps that attach to the bottle's rim; the chanciest rely on a rubber or cork finger that is forced into the mouth).

These civilized refinements are a far cry from Ernest Hemingway's bota, a beaten-up Spanish goatskin or leather canteen that when squeezed shot a stream of rustic vino tinto into his mouth. (One-liter botas, decorative when hung in cellars, and usable, can still be purchased, from army and navy stores and camping-supply companies.)

To keep white wine and Champagne properly chilled, a sizable metal ice bucket, a cooler, is indispensable, and, as host, if you are pouring it does not hurt to have a restaurant stand for the bucket next to you (with a handily placed towel to prevent dripping). Inexpensive metal buckets and stands are found in kitchen- and restaurant-supply outlets. (A tip: a bucket filled with a mixture of half ice and half water will chill wine faster than ice alone.)

Terra-cotta coolers, which are soaked in water and then chilled in the refrigerator, bring earthiness to the table: as the water evaporates from the porous clay, the wine bottle is cooled. Marble coolers, in white, green and black colors, and chilled before being positioned on the table, may be equally appealing. I prefer the double-walled clear-acrylic cylinder-shaped kind. Some consumers like the chrome Rapid Ice, a sleeve kept in the freezer that chills still wine and Champagne in minutes and keeps both cold for about three hours.

A product called Vin Chilla that electrically circulates iced water around bottles in a container to chill them in four minutes, and warm water around cellar-chilled reds to bring them to room temperature, is receiving favorable attention. I have not used it but expect to give it a try.

Through a Glass, Lightly

No modern wine accessories transcend decanters in beauty. By modern, I mean the curvaceous, clear-glass, unetched, uncut variety—unetched because the eye wants to appreciate undistracted the wine's color and relationship to the surrounding glass.

First things first: decanters are about wine; wine is not about decanters. Decanters should not displace bottles from the table. The bottles should be present for their label information throughout a meal.

A full-scale cellar wants shelves, even cabinets, to exhibit decanters, but not to treat them as don't-touch-me museum pieces: To have is to hold; to hold is to use. And to use is to aerate and to separate old wines from their sediment.

The human spirit responds to pouring, whether on the scale of a few ounces or of Niagara Falls; the personal act implies generosity and sharing. It's a pretty sight, too.

In its literature, Riedel, the great Austrian glassworks, quotes Christian Moueix, the proprietor of Château Pétrus, in Pomerol, as having said, eloquently I think, that decanting "is a sign of respect for old wines and a sign of confidence in young wines." His logic is this: "Decanting old wines, just a few minutes before they are served, helps to ensure that the wines' clarity and brilliance are not obscured by any deposit that may have developed over time. Decanting young wines several hours before they are served gives the wine a chance to bloom and attain a stage of development that normally requires years of aging."

In judging and buying decanters and their juniors, carafes—in fact, all wine crystal ware—think lightness. Why it is so I cannot say, but, psychologically, seemingly weightless glass focuses one's attention on and enhances appreciation of its contents, and heavy, clunky glass calls undue, partly distracting attention to these structural liabilities. If you cannot afford upscale merchandise, no big deal: decant into a pitcher or into a wine bottle washed in hot, soap-free water. The wine bottle itself can be a decanter. Pour off a glass, recork carefully and repeatedly turn the bottle upside down; it is perhaps crude, even uncouth, but it works.

Decanting serves three ends: heightening wine's aesthetic appearance; aerating—oxygenating—wine so as to soften its tannic roughness and hasten the development of its bouquet and flavors; and separating wine from deposits of sediment that hefty and older reds and dessert reds like port and Madeira throw.

Certain delicate aged and delicate young wines transferred into another vessel too far in advance of drinking may experience diminution of their character, freshness and fruit. The practice of opening a bottle and letting it stand and "breathe" for a short time is a nonstarter: the small amount of air interacting with the tiny surface area of wine in the neck has a negligible effect on development. Some critics shun decanting, arguing that swirling wine in a glass yields superior results.

Why blight graceful decanters with pretentious metalwork, the decorative descendant of England's so-called claret jugs of the 19th century? Lumpish pewter legs and baroque decorations, lids and handles contradict the Bacchic spirit. I much prefer to have the eyes' appetites teased by the pure, sexy balletic curves and bends, the glints and refractions of the glass.

But, unaccountably, I love toys like metal aerating funnels (holding removable mesh particle-trapping screens) with pinholes and spiral stems, as well as crystal versions that, as if micro-fountains, enliven wine by sending it cascading gently down decanters' interior walls.

To whet an appetite for ornate, museum-level decanters called claret jugs, visit www.claretjugs.com, an annotated Web site sponsored by Richard Kent, the president and chief executive officer of a holding company in Chicago. Silver-mounted glass claret jugs, used for various kinds of wine despite their name (claret is a British synonym for red Bordeaux), first appeared in England in the 1830s and caught on in the affluent classes. These once-fashionable and now rare examples of the conflation of the glassmakers' and silversmiths' arts can be bought at auction and from specialists in antiques.

My favorite decanters have tall, slender goose necks and bulbous bottoms that can hold a pond of wine bathed by air. As in stemware, the principal brands to know are Riedel, the Austrian manufacturer, whose name is a byword in wine ranks thanks to years of heavy advertising and promotion, and Spiegelau, the German manufacturer, who reports making inroads on Riedel sales in the United States, especially in restaurants.

In selecting decanters, questions that can be answered only on the basis of personal need arise: Should I get what is reputed to be best and is most expensive, or are differences in grade so small as to be insignificant? Should I get a regular bottle-size or a magnum-size? Should it be a more or less traditional vertical design or one of the variations on the endearing, sleek birdlike design? And, since lead is a potential health danger, should I get lead-free glass?

Indeed, California takes lead so seriously that an Internet glassware ad by K & L Wine Merchants of Redwood City and San Francisco (www.klwines.com) carried a warning under Proposition 65, enacted in 1986, saying that "consuming foods or beverages that have been kept or served in leaded crystal products will expose you to lead, a chemical known . . . to cause birth defects or other reproductive harm."

After a Columbia University study in 1991 found that wine and spirits leached lead from crystal decanters and wine glasses, the Food and Drug Administration recommended that beverages not be stored in crystal for long periods and that lead crystal not be used daily. If you have a glass of wine daily, the F.D.A. said, do not drink it from a crystal goblet.

In the relatively low-cost category of decanters, my preferences are Wine Enthusiast's 48-ounce Italian-made Visual decanter, which features a dome in the punt, or bottom, that promotes oxygenation, and the 60-ounce, lead-free Spiegelau Vivendi model. Minimally, purchasers of modern decanters should review the entire output of Riedel, all the Spiegelau versions (made in Germany by Nachtmann) and the output of Rosenthal (also German).

Although my at-home experience with Spiegelau stemware is very limited, the restaurant world's view of the brand seems increasingly favorable. While many sommeliers concede that, comparatively, wines may taste truer to intended form in the appropriate Riedels, they maintain that the difference is small and is offset by cheaper Spiegelau prices and greater strength in resisting breakage, especially during dishwashing. The brand is used in the ever-busy Morrell Wine Bar and Cafe, at Restaurant Daniel and at Lutèce in New York.

In the Spiegelau line, the Authentis series is touted as if were Nachtmann's answer to the best that Riedel has to offer, the Sommelier line, although the angularity in certain Authentis glasses more nearly resembles the design found in Riedel's Vinum Extreme series. The Spiegelau Vino Grande, intended for hard-knocks everyday use with minimal sacrifice of wine appreciation, is the series customarily found in restaurants and in retail stores.

If a rich man is most daunted by the prospect of getting into heaven, it's because he has never faced an even harder task: cleaning a decanter. One way to avoid this thankless chore, to keep the crystal spot-free, is to acquire a drying stand. The best I've found, in an IWA catalog, has a pan to catch the drips from the upside down vessel.

(By the way, the single best way to clean wine glasses, if you have an eternity of free time, is to steam them clean with distilled water and wipe them dry with a lint-free cloth. I do not think you will thank me for this tip.)

One beloved decanter, displayed in my dining room for 18 years, is a hand-blown glass porrón, a communal vessel that vaguely resembles a goatskin bag and is found throughout Spain (it holds olive oil, too). It is filled at the top, and a thin stream of wine is poured—into your mouth or a glass—from an upward-pointing spout midway in the base. No glasses are needed for anyone. Beware, you may get a face full of wine until you get the hang of it.

Where to buy such items? Nationwide, virtually all merchants, large and small, who specialize in glassware or who maintain glassware departments will display a range of offerings, typically small. But nothing rivals the Internet for speed and amplitude in providing a dense concentration of shapes, sizes and styles along with technical information, and the rivalry in prices is breathtaking—a short course that could be called Free Market 101.

Those familiar with mail-order houses' catalogs know the panorama of merchandise, from kitsch through the sublime, available to the aficionado. Wine lovers are likely to find in these tempting, frequently arriving mailings all the wares they need, or may want to need (especially at holiday gift-giving time, when Possession Fever virtually breaks the thermometer).

But these catalogs need not define the whole search. Increasingly I rely on the search capabilities of Google on the Internet in all realms of information. By merely asking Google to find "wine decanters," for example, in seconds the screen presents a cornucopia of possibilities. In the wine-gadget sphere, such fact- and price-finding missions are limited only by one's imagination.

Observant wine lovers have long known that the size, contours, thickness, weight and delicacy of stemware influence one's perception and enjoyment of wine. The Riedel revolution lies both in the technical analysis and insightful exposition by Claus, père, and Georg, fils, of why and how this is so, and in their stemware shapes that cater to the physiology of the nose and palate.

By contrast, far too many fancy crystal glasses in bridal-registry shops are anti-wine—as are astonishingly clunky glasses in upscale restaurants—and are dedicated solely to advertising an income level. If you have noticed that crystal ware brands that are the bread-and-butter darlings of bridal registries—Waterford, Christofle, Wedgwood, Lalique, Orrefors, Royal Copenhagen, Lenox—are absent here, it is because I cannot brook their overdone designs, and, gauging from their absence in informed debate about wine ware, neither can other wine aficionados.

Stemware from Riedel Glas, as the company is called, teaches (or reducates) us to grasp—to interpret—winemakers' intentions and terroir more fully, and how to do so. Further, it exposes producers' shoddiness and hype pitilessly. In short, Georg Riedel's standard-setting brand is synonymous with informed consumer investment, rigorous connnoisseurship, seasoned hedonism and the Bauhaus esthetic of function dictating form.

With 56 specialized wine glasses in the catalog, does Riedel risk over-fastidiousness? Who can afford and store so many? Who needs a possible Riedel that caters only to pinot blanc from the Willamette Valley of Oregon? Riedel himself said six glasses met his fundamental needs.

"You should spend for one glass what you spend for one bottle of wine," Riedel said. This means that if your budget permits only low-priced wines, you may enjoy them generously, and if one is in blue-chip territory, you may relish them exponentially.

Riedel was spending a few days in Manhattan in 2002, and his representative offered me Riedel's regular mini-course in comparative tasting. A chardonnay,

sauvignon blanc, pinot noir and cabernet sauvignon are sampled in standard restaurant glassware and then in Riedel crystal explicitly designed to highlight each wine's characteristic features.

No, thank you, I replied: Since I use several Riedel glasses at home for reviewing, I have mastered that knowledge. Rather, I asked that Riedel illustrate in tiny detail the subtle ways a riesling and a pinot noir can differently reveal their kaleidoscopic facets in the variously priced Riedel glasses created precisely for them.

To my surprise, Georg Riedel said that outside his glass factory, in the village of Kufstein, Austria, such an across-the-board "rainbow" tasting had never occurred. He welcomed the idea—graciously, I thought, because inevitably the undertaking would expose not only strengths but also comparative weaknesses in his wares.

At our tasting, at the Manhattan restaurant Montrachet, with five partly filled glasses facing us, I asked Riedel, "Which is the wine?" He paused a long second, then replied: "Indeed! Which is the wine?"

We knew the Austrian white under scrutiny: Leo Alzinger's 1999 Loibner Frauenweingarten grüner veltliner. Our questions were code words for basic issues: How might Alzinger, an outstanding producer in the Wachau Valley, have wanted us to experience and understand this wine? And how well did the Riedel glassware cater to Alzinger's intentions? Which glass, if any, got it just right? (Obviously, with Alzinger not present, we could not know definitively.)

In addition to pouring the Alzinger, Bernard Sun, Montrachet's imperturbable head sommelier, gave us the great F. X. Pichler's 1996 Loibner Klostersatz grüner veltliner.

We tasted the whites in Riedel's Vinum Extreme series riesling glass ($28 each), Vinum series sauvignon blanc glass ($22.50), Vinum riesling grand cru glass ($19.90), Vinum Rheingau glass ($19.90) and Ouverture series white—wine glass ($9.90).

In the Vinum Extreme glass, which is diamond-shaped, the Alzinger had a beautiful aroma, its oiliness (a favorable characteristic) stood out, and it was smooth: "Full expression of the wine," my notes say. In the Vinum sauvignon blanc glass, where it was inappropriate, it was offputtingly dense. In the Vinum riesling grand cru glass, its floral perfume was outstanding, and the wine was marvelous. The Vinum Rheingau glass was too heavy in my hand, and its dead weight weakened my interest in the wine. In the inexpensive Ouverture glass, the wine was light and lean; my notes say the glass is "beautifully balanced—nice in the hand—friendly."

The pinot noirs chosen were Simon Bize's 1997 Savigny-lès-Beaune Aux Vergelesses and Jean Grivot's Vosne-Romanée Les Beaux Monts, both Premiers Crus. Both went into the top-of-the-line Sommeliers series Burgundy grand cru glass ($89), Vinum Extreme series pinot noir glass ($30) and the Vinum series Burgundy glass ($24.90).

Oddly, the Bize tasted dull in the $89 glass; the pinot noir character stood out in the $30; it was best in the $24.90 glass. How is that for bang for the buck? "They are different wines," Riedel said. "No grape is so sensitive to glass as pinot noir." My notes say, "The differences are so bold as to be shocking."

Georg Riedel, a fan of fruit, preferred the Grivot in the $89 glass. I love funkiness—barnyard character—in red Burgundy, and it stood out best in the $24.90 glass. How's that for making debris of Absolute Pronouncements about Wine No. 1?

A Pantry
and a Sink

A properly stocked wine cellar should have a small pantry. Here's why: You've acquired surprisingly low-priced Burgundies at auction. Since wine is about sharing, you've invited novices and aficionados to sample a dozen; after an hour, the bottles and guests will go to the dinner table. But problems lie ahead: they will find successive wines harder to appreciate at the tasting as tannins, acidity and alcohol builds up on their palates.

To solve this famous problem, wine teachers and sponsors of professional tastings provide sparkling and still water, baguette slices, Carr's water crackers or cheese. But when James Trezise, president of the New York Wine and Grape Foundation, a trade association based in the beautiful and underappreciated Finger Lakes wine region, judged wines at the Los Angeles County Fair, he found something new. Accompanying the cheese cubes and crackers, he said, were "the most delightful olives I've ever had," which were "regardless of the wine—red or white—the best palate cleanser I've ever had."

Curious, I obtained cans from the source, the C. C. Graber Company, California olive merchants since 1894. Bull's-eye! Graber's cured olives, tree ripened in the San Joaquin Valley, outrank the choicest Spanish olives I've ever tried with fresh fino and manzanilla sherries (which, in my view, are the world's greatest and least valued whites). Greenish, reddish-green and brownish-green, Graber olives are nutty, smooth, mellow, succulently meaty, but not filling. Paradoxically, eaten warm they not only neutralized the palate but also heightened the pleasures of the succeeding reds and whites sipped. Look for No. 12 size olives in 7.5-ounce cans with a flat 1940s appearance. Graber is at 315 East Fourth Street, Ontario, California, 91764; Web: www.graberolives.com.

Uninterested in the ceremonial or ritual practices of wine opening, some aficionados prefer to clean, uncork and sample their bottles, and sometimes decant them, out of sight of guests and family. Truth to tell, the mechanics can turn a little sloppy: cork crumbles into the wine and must be decanted out; a few drops slide down the side of the bottle, threatening an heirloom white linen tablecloth and a wifely rebuke after the guests have departed; despite gingerly handling, Champagne may spout from the bottle when it pops open (I have seen it happen in the hands of one of the world's most celebrated and suave producers).

Although installation of a well-lighted sink is not often recommended, a partitioned sink with hot and cold water faucets comes in handy, especially if it has an adjacent counter that can hold a few bottles and a stemware drying rack (with a small waste container on the floor underneath for paper towels, corks, foil, etc.) Make sure to close faucets fully to minimize their effect on the cellar's humidity. The counter, or a cabinet below, can be used to house glass and decanter washing brushes and containers of liquid cleansing solutions. If you use a silver tastevin to check the color, clarity and health of the wine before serving it, the device can be washed and hung by its chain at the counter.

The sommelier work done, the evening's wine can be carried to the table or into the party room in a metal bottle tote (the kind milkmen once used). Or the filled flute glasses, when Champagne is served, can be distributed from a hand-carried tray.

Striking
Gold at Auction

The world is awash in great personal cellars, with, every once and a while, a mind-boggling one suddenly breaking surface in auction rooms. Morrell & Company astonished even jaded collectors with an $8 million 2,384-lot collection that sold partly, for $5,197,337, over two days at the Four Seasons Restaurant in Manhattan. It was the largest sum realized in an American auction in 2002.

Morrell declined to identify the consignor, but wine industry sources identified him as Georges Marciano of Beverly Hills, California, a designer and co-founder of Guess? Inc., the jeans company.

In the catalog, Peter Morrell, chairman of Morrell Fine Wine Auctions, gave this passionate description of encountering the cellar for the first time:

"In the 1930's, when the notorious bank robber Willie Sutton was asked, 'Why do you rob banks?' he replied, 'Because that's where the money is!' Sutton's famous line popped into my head when I flew into LAX and whisked off to Beverly Hills to meet with a possible auction consignor located in a former bank building. There, a subterranean combination-locked three-foot-thick 10,000-pound bank vault door ever so slowly swung open to reveal—not piles of cash—but a king's treasure of millions of dollars' worth of fine wine—including thousands of perfect original wooden cases from all of the top Bordeaux vineyards: Château Ausone, Cheval Blanc, Haut-Brion, Lafite, Latour, Mouton, Margaux and Pétrus, stacked high to the ceiling! As the vault door opened, a cool breeze rushed out and—light-headed with excitement—I rushed in!

"When, to my continuing amazement, five additional air-cooled rooms were unlocked in this labyrinthine Wilshire Boulevard cellar, as each new door opened I began to feel a serious tingle of anticipation, much like I imagine Dashiell Hammett's "fat man" must have felt when he first held what he believed to be the original Maltese Falcon!"

One feels dazed surveying the catalog: six columns of listings of Château Ducru-Beaucaillou, in various sizes and formats from 1970 to 1996; nearly eight columns devoted to Château Pichon-Longueville, Comtesse de Lalande from 1958 to 1996; 19 columns of Lafite-Rothschild from 1928 to 1996; and nearly 19 columns of Château Pétrus from 1945 to 1996. Many were housed in their original wooden cases—owc's, as auction lingo puts it.

Morrell was perhaps not exaggerating when it described the contents of the sale as "a once-in-a-lifetime offering of the finest Bordeaux in pristine condition." Its enthusiastic language was appropriate in the recitation of goodies: "1900, 1928, 1945, 1961 Léoville-Poyferré Imperials, three Jeroboams of 1970 Montrose, a case of 1959 Grand-Puy-Lacoste" along with an "unusual Marie-Jeanne of 1949 La Conseillante, magnums of timelessly thick 1926 Haut-Brion." This kind of trove makes collectors drool.

In the late 1990's, the center of gravity in the auctioning of fine and rare wines in brick-and-mortar establishments shifted from London to America, with New York City at the center. An overlay of proliferating Internet wine-auction establishments has reinforced America's primacy in the field. This concentration affords novice and seasoned collectors alike yearlong opportunities to buy wine not only for immediate drinking but also for cellaring for future use and for reselling in the secondary market. Like all plunges into investments, wine acquisitions at auction require systematic homework.

The starting point is a listing of all the houses that hold auctions. In

New York State, by law independent auction houses that want to sell wine must have as a partner a wine merchant who has held a state license for at least a decade.

In New York, the auction businesses are: Acker, Merrall & Condit, a wine merchant on the West Side of Manhattan; Morrell & Company, which has a spiffy store and also a cafe and wine bar in Rockefeller Center; NYWines/Christie's, a team in which the merchant is New York Wine Warehouse, a boutique operation in Long Island City, just across the East River from Manhattan; Sotheby's/Aulden Cellars, with the retail store on the ground floor of Sotheby's headquarters on the East Side of Manhattan; and Zachys, a wine emporium in Scarsdale, an affluent commuters' suburb in nearby Westchester County.

In Chicago, interest centers on Edward Roberts International, a boutique house that went into business in 2002, and the Chicago Wine Company. On the West Coast, Butterfields, in San Francisco, bears watching; long in the doldrums, it was purchased in 2002 by Bonhams, the British house, and is being reinvigorated. (NYWines/Christie's holds sales in Los Angeles.)

And in London, Sotheby's and Christie's hold regular sales; in 2002, Christie's held its first auctions in Paris.

At auctions you may buy wines for less than retail prices, and bid for wines that are no longer found in stores or, like the California cult wines sold from mailing lists, that seldom if ever reach stores. For example, on Dec. 7, 2002, when a case of 1990 Château Gruaud-Larose, a Second Growth Bordeaux, estimated at $600 to $800, sold at Zachys' auction, which was held in Restaurant Daniel in Manhattan, for $1,276, or $106.33 a bottle, Sherry-Lehmann, a carriage-trade merchant a five-minute walk away, was offering the case in its catalog for $119.95 a bottle, or $1,439.40 a case. That day, Zachys sold six bottles of 1989 Château

Haut-Brion, a Bordeaux First Growth, for $3,016 or $502.67 a bottle, while Sherry-Lehmann was charging $675 for that very bottle. Of course, Sherry-Lehmann could persuasively argue that, at that price level, the premium paid to offset the risk built into acquiring second-hand goods ensured pristine quality. If, however, an auction house has misperceived the quality of a consignment that is a bust, or did not accurately describe it, the buyer may have negotiating power. Auction houses go out of their way to avoid having disgruntled customers.

You should decide in advance of bidding whether you are buying to drink, or to hold and sell, and what you are willing to pay; otherwise, drawn into the quickly rising fever of a bidding war and its ego- or id-driven challenges, you may wind up stuck with consignments you had never intended to acquire.

Some catalogs contain crucial information about the condition and provenance (ownership and storage history) of each lot of wines, along with tasting notes by established critics. Attention must be paid. Houses inspect cellars to establish the condition of the wines, often rejecting holdings that have not been subject to temperature and humidity controls or that, for various reasons, sometimes intuited up by seasoned auctioneers' instincts, seem iffy. (The analogy in the newspaper business is a hoary, grammar-school-level axiom passed along to novice reporters: when in doubt, leave it out.) The more owners' hands that consignments have passed through, the higher the risk to buyers.

The following clause from Edward Roberts International's catalog suggest what buyers are up against: "Neither we nor the consignor make any representation or warranty of any kind, express or implied, with respect to any of the following characteristics of the property: age, authenticity, genuineness, attribution, provenance, physical condition, importance, size, quality, quantity, rarity, value, historical references or significance, material, source or origin."

Welcome to the roulette table.

You do not have to buy blindly. Auction houses encourage viewing, by appointment. As the NYWines/Christie's catalog declares: "Pre-auction viewings are open to the public and free of charge. Christie's specialists are available to give advice at views or by appointment. We encourage prospective buyers to examine lots thoroughly and to request condition reports." Usually auctions are preceded, that day or a day earlier, by hourlong tastings, for which reservations must be paid and a nominal fee paid. A bottle of or two of some of the best lots are opened, and you can judge for yourself whether the quality merits a bid. The cross-section of blue-chip wines available makes such tastings one of the great bargains in the wine world. Even if you are not a bidder, if you reserve a spot early and are in line when the door opens, you are ready for piercing insights into an array of wines that otherwise may be financially out of reach.

In auctions, wines are sold "as is"—in other words, caveat emptor: pretty much every lot dealt is a gamble. That is why players should carefully study the terms and conditions of sales set forth in quasi-legalese in catalogs. To counteract the risks built into "as is," neophytes should practice an "as if" strategy—that is, before buying at auction, acquire a catalog (they can be obtained by subscription), select a batch of wines to buy theoretically, calculate the maximum prices they are prepared to pay, attend the auction and participate on a make-believe basis, and, afterward digest the costs and lessons of this dry run.

Catalogs contain high and low estimates of the probable selling price of collectible wines, usually based on prices recently fetched by the house or other houses. Another way to keep relatively abreast of movements of prices for blue-chip wines is to consult indexes found in *Decanter* magazine (updated monthly) and its Web site, www.decanter.com, both based in London, and in *Wine Spectator* (the data are published quarterly) and www.winespectator.com.

Decanter magazine's Fine Wine Price Watch covers superior Bordeaux vintages from 1961 through 1996, red Burgundy from 1960 through 1990, white Burgundy from 1961 through 1990 and port from 1927 through 1994; readers must convert the pounds to dollars. And www.decanter.com's Fine Wine Tracker extensively lists red wines from Australia, Bordeaux, Burgundy, California and Italy, white Bordeaux and vintage port; it bases its data on pound prices realized at Christie's and Sotheby's in Britain, and dollar prices realized in America by Christie's, Sotheby's and Morrell & Company.

Wine Spectator's Auction Index leans heavily on Bordeaux, then handfuls of representative California and Italian wines, and ports. A far lengthier index, with French and Italian regions, Spain, California, Oregon and Washington is found on www.winespectator.com.

Buyers will also pay a commission or premium, usually around 15 percent of the so-called hammer price; other costs, like delivery charges, insurance fees and sales taxes may come into play.

Behind virtually all wines brought to auction are reserves: prices, confidentially set by the seller and the house, under which the wine cannot be sold. It may hover at about 25 percent under the low pre-sale estimate. Wines that do not meet the reserve are, in auction lingo, "passed" or "bought in." After the auction, the purchase price of wines that found no buyers may be negotiable. (When lots are not subject to a reserve, they may be denoted by a symbol like a star or triangle.)

Generally, auctions can be dull, with occasional spirited bidding wars that bring the rooms alive and spark applause. Bidders physically present and raising their numbered paddles fast have an advantage over online bidders and those who place bids by mail and fax. This is especially true after the early lots of a wine are sold and duplicate versions come up late in the afternoon, when alertness decreases and fatigue rises; it is not uncommon, though it seems irrational, that multiple consignments of exactly the same wine, appearing and reappearing throughout an auction, can all sell at differing, sometimes widely differing, prices. Another benefit of being present is the opportunity to bid for so-called parcels— that is, often when many identical lots follow each other, the first winning bidder is allowed to buy the remainder at the same price.

The Pleasures
of Catalogs

For some auctiongoers, the catalogs may be as interesting as a rural telephone book. Others may find them decorative, in an almost coffee-table-book way, and addictively worth saving, likes years' accumulations of *Gourmet* and *National Geographic* magazines.

Aside from being quasi-textbooks—study them long enough and you learn what wines are really good—catalogs occasionally are virtually works of art in themselves. The color photographs of sales' marquee bottles are artful, striking, breathtaking and, though it hardly seems possible, can be virtually original in composition.

A Morrell 2002 catalog devoted a page to three abutting bottles of Turley Wine Cellars's rare 2000 White Coat from San Luis Obispo County, California. Golden, centrally lit as if by a molten setting sun, seen from an angle, they linger in the imagination for hours. NYWines/Christie's, as the house has named its partnership with the New York Wine Warehouse, took luminosity further in a catalog for a 2002 Los Angeles sale: against a black background, seven horizontally aligned bottles of golden 1989 Château d'Yquem swathed in white tissue paper (and fronted by a crystalline unwrapped bottle) are turned simultaneously into candles and candlewicks by fiery back lighting.

There is something winningly mesmerizing about allowing one's eyes to march up and down the pages, column after column, reading sound-bite size comments on the wines by the likes of such authorities and luminaries as the critic Robert M. Parker Jr.; Michael Broadbent, who has long been identified with Christie's and is author, most recently, of "Michael Broadbent's Vintage Wine: Fifty Years of Tasting Three Centuries of Wine"; and Serena Sutcliffe, the head of Sotheby's International Wine Department.

Who could, for example, resist Ms. Sutcliffe's notes, in a Sotheby's/Aulden Cellars catalog, for the 1992 Chevalier Montrachet from Domaine Leflaive: "Hedonistic heaven. I truly think this is one of the great white Burgundies ever—especially at this stage of its life. Now mature and ready to drink. *Carpe diem!*" (Actually, everybody resisted it; the case, estimated at $4,000 to $5,500, did not sell, possibly because of the description: "5 signs of seepage. 1 slightly stained vintage neck label." People much prefer virginal condition.)

Talk about the romance of wine! The cover of Sotheby's catalog for a Dec. 4, 2002, sale in London shows dirty bottles with soiled, stained labels of a 1921 Schloss Reinhartshausen Erbacher Rheinhell riesling (in the Rheingau) and a 1900 Château Lafite. Along with them are two drinking glasses, partly filled with a brick-colored wine, and bearing a royal crest. A prefatory explanation tells us that "wines from the German castle of Schloss Falkenstein came from a hidden room no more than one and a half meters high." The wine, we learn, "was hidden by Lothar Graf von der Asserburg-Falkenstein-Rothkirch, in advance of the invading Russians, before he fled the castle in 1944." Who could bear to part with a catalog that unfolds the fascinating story of their recovery?

In overusing "legendary," the hype that drives wine marketing devalues the truly legendary. But NYWines/Christie's resurrects it, in a June 2002 catalog, in Broadbent's anecdote about discovering, in Glamis Castle, Scotland, "a bin in which there were 42 magnums of 1870 Lafite with original wax seals." The 13th Earl of Strathmore had bought them in 1878. "The wine was so astringent that he did not like it, and when he died . . . the wine was virtually untouched,"

Broadbent went on. "It took a full 50 years to become mellow enough to drink, and it was already a century old at the time of my visit." Later, he tasted it several times over the years, and concluded, "It is quite simply one of the greatest-ever clarets." Sharing that experience vicariously, perhaps during bedtime reading, can only arouse envy. (Glamis Castle, incidentally, was the childhood home of the Queen Mother, who died in 2002 at 101, and the legendary setting of Shakespeare's *Macbeth*.)

Except on the rare occasions when a cellar being sold is so celebrated that the parties think that publicizing their names will add cachet to the event and dollars to prices, consignors and buyers are not identified by the fiercely protective auction houses. A rare example was Zachys' inaugural auction, which after opening with a lot whose source was described in discreet language, "Property of a Great Connoisseur," then moved on to "A Spectacular Collection of Original Cases of Classic Bordeaux," directly from the cellars of Mähler-Besse, an old-line Bordeaux trading company. Later on, "Treasures from the Scandia Cellar" identified the property of Mr. and Mrs. Robert E. Petersen of Los Angeles, whose once-celebrated restaurant, Scandia, has long been closed.

A Sotheby's/Aulden Cellars catalog characterized one consignment as the "Wines of a St. Louis Gentleman," and another lot, "highly desirable cult California wines," as the "Property of a New York Gentleman." I don't doubt that gentlemen live in St. Louis: T. S. Eliot was born there. Once, perhaps twice, in 36 years' residence I have been introduced to gentlemen in New York. But when I encountered "Property of a New Jersey Gentleman," I felt the house had been gulled: in my home state, the last known gentleman was Woodrow Wilson.

Golden Oldies

Wine antiques, which turn up at auctions, as well as antique vineyard implements, provide visual relief for cellar owners who, while enchanted by the appearance of massed bottles in trellised shelving, from time to time sense a certain tedium in the patterns.

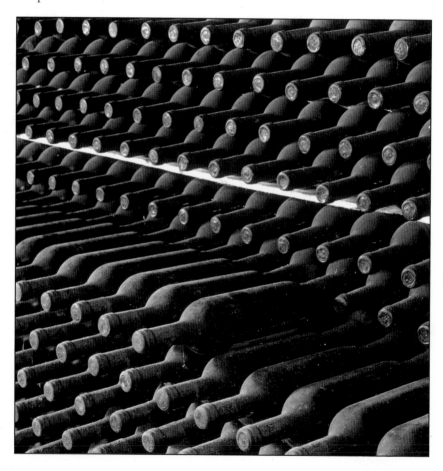

One does not rush into antiques purchases, of course. For example, at a Sotheby's sale of Americana in 2001, a wine cup made by John Hull and Robert Sanderson Sr. of Boston around 1660 brought $775,750, well above the $300,000 high estimate. It was loaned to the Metropolitan Museum of Art and may wind up there as a gift.

When Western wine artifacts are balanced by those from Asia, furnished cellars become vastly more interesting. They might include Chinese and Japanese wine jars, bronze wine vessels, wine kettles and ladles and wine tables.

If you had been flush at a 2002 auction held by Phillips, de Pury & Luxembourg in Manhattan, you might have bought a wine cistern once owned by Baron Alfred de Rothschild, a member of the family's British house. Carved about 1700 from a solid block of dark red marble from Languedoc, in France, it weighs half a ton. The oval rim was decorated with two huge gilded ram's heads. Estimated at $150,000 to $200,000, it sold for $151,000.

Incidentally, if you collect (or merely admire) wine antiques, pay a leisurely visit to the Metropolitan Museum of Art in New York City and discipline your eyes to search out, insofar as possible, only artworks—paintings, sculptures, metalwork, carvings, glassware, etc.—that contain wine and grape motifs. If, at the outset, you are skeptical, as I was, wondering how much material you would find, you will soon be deluged by the offerings from the ancient world (no surprise) through modernity. I once spent a 40-hour week walking through the entire museum looking for these motifs, and found them in virtually every department. I left with a vastly enriched understanding of how the vine has twined itself through and around secular and religious civilization—from Dionysian frolics to regal banquets to holy communion to the Passover seder.

When a Co-Pilot Is Needed

Regular auctiongoers in Manhattan often see a heavy-set man sitting in an advantageous position, usually in the rear of the room, where the broad field of bidders and their paddle-waving can be closely observed. With him is an auction catalog, heavily color-tabbed and notated, a handful of numbered paddles, a supply of pens and a cellphone at hand. Patiently, lot-by-lot, he records the hammer prices and paddle numbers of the successful buyers.

He is Kevin A. Swersey, a partner in and co-president of a small Manhattan firm called the Connoisseur's Advisory Group, which provides consulting and management services for high-net-worth collectors of fine wine and art. (He also holds the title of senior adviser in the Zachys auction team.) At auctions, he represents clients, bidding for them and keeping them informed of floor action. Noting the hammer prices and paddle numbers of successful buyers helps him to establish trends in the marketplace.

A Group spokesman says that it "advises a select clientele of wine connoisseurs throughout the Americas and Europe who are dedicated to developing and maintaining wine collections of the highest quality." The firm does not advertise and has no Web site. The client base, whose confidentiality and privacy are maintained, comes only from referrals from existing clients.

"Fees are based upon the needs and desires of each individual client," Swersey said. "Clients have diverse needs. Some want to start a collection from scratch. Others have no idea what they have, and want an inventory conducted to put their collections in perspective. We have clients that have residences all over the world, and want to have a selection of wines readily available, whether at their ski house in the Rockies or their yacht cruising the Mediterranean. They rely on us to assist them, whether it means bringing in a team to build a new wine cellar, arranging to have their valuable collections insured properly, even assisting with the securing of temperature-controlled transportation from purchase to destination."

When purchasing for a client, the company acts as its representative not only at auctions but also in communicating with wine suppliers worldwide. It also handles wine sales on behalf of clients. A decision to sell may be undertaken for many reasons, including ownership of too many of the same wines, reduced consumption for health reasons, etc. After various means of disposition, including auction and private sale, are discussed, the firm handles all the negotiations and logistics, including financial settlement.

"For some clients," Swersey said, "we take an annual physical inventory, which helps us to monitor consumption and advise on future acquisition programs. Last December, for example, I drove to North Bergen, N. J., to the warehouse of Western Carriers, a major independent wine storage facility. It offers the best temperature-controlled moving service available. I spent several hours examining some lots purchased as on-the-spot decisions at a recent New York auction. I confirmed that the wine was in proper condition and as described in the catalog It is always better to catch discrepancies prior to the payment and movement of wine. Then I shifted to another project, confirming that a palette (50 cases) of wine was correctly consolidated before it was trucked to a client's house. Many collectors host world-class wine dinners, as venues for sharing with like-minded individuals. Some of these dinners take up to a year to pull together."

There is a time to buy wines, and a time to sell them, a time to create a cellar, and a time to divest. Three d's govern the time to divest: death, divorce and

disaster. And that is a time when it is desirable, or necessary, to turn to a seasoned wine appraiser, a specialist who can assess the value of your cellar and guide you in disposing of it, whether wholly at once or fractionally.

One of the keenest in the business is William H. Edgerton of Darien, Connecticut, who has been evaluating cellars nationwide since 1987. He also consults for wine buyers and sellers. Edgerton has compiled what he calls "the world's largest wine sales database," containing more than 650,000 entries. He originated, owned and published part of that database annually from 1989 to 1999 as the Wine Price File, "the largest available listing of retail and auction prices of wine in print," he said. While he has sold it to Wine Technologies, he remains the editor, and the publication was renamed Edgerton's Wine Price File.

"There are three types of value usually appropriate for wine collections," Edgerton explains. "Net liquidation value: the amount a seller would net from a sale of wine in a commercial wine auction. Replacement value: the cost of replacing the wine with like bottles, but not including the entrepreneurial cost of the time to do the search and make the purchases. And fair market value: the probable price for which the wine could be sold in an arm's-length transaction between a willing and knowledgeable buyer and seller."

"The specific basis for valuation of wine is market data and comparable sales. No other valuation techniques are appropriate for use with wine. The primary sources of comparable sales are the principal fine wine auctions in the United States, in England and in Europe.

"A wine appraiser is a professional who, like other appraisers, charges by the hour for his time," Edgerton said. "The hourly rate may be affected by whether or not the work is done only in his office, or if time must be spent inventorying a collection." An appraiser, he continued, "can also quote a dollar cost to appraise each wine listed on an inventory (not each bottle), and that cost varies by the type of wine being appraised, with some Italian and German wines carrying a premium and singletons or low-value wines carrying a discount. With a cost per wine known in advance, the total cost of the appraisal can be calculated in advance, which is not possible when hourly charges are quoted."

Buying Smarts

Economic purchasing to stock the cellar is helped by acquiring the habit of thinking in multiples of six: half cases, full cases, one and one-half cases, etc. The reason is that discounts sometimes kick in at six bottles, and are a standard practice at 12. Ask if magnum (1.5 liter) versions of wines you like exist, and compare the price with the 750-milliliter bottling to see if savings are possible (not always); check, too, on discounts for buying multiples of magnums.

Although half bottles (375-milliliter) bottles tend to cost more than half the price of a full bottle, if you lose money relatively by buying one you still save money absolutely: if the half-bottle is fresh merchandise (you have to trust the merchant), it may enable you to learn whether you'll like the standard size. (The premium you pay in restaurants for half bottles is offset by the opportunity afforded for versatile drinking in multicourse meals.) Routinely ask the store manager or owner about whether they have any unpublicized specials and if special discounts may be available on any end-of-bin items.

Save your receipts when buying, and if a bottle is tainted return it immediately. Enlightened merchants will replace it and be given a credit by their suppliers.

Bottles for the Long Haul

Serious collecting involves an ever-deepening awareness of what counts and what does not. No matter what your preferences are now, and will become, remember that nothing surpasses the importance of buying only good vintages from long-established major sources if you plan years and years of storage.

Although places like Australia, Argentina, Chile, New Zealand, South Africa as well as Washington, Oregon, New York State and Virginia are coming on strong, by and large (there are exceptions) they have not graduated into the blue-chip vin de garde (wine for keeping) class.

France is the mother lode of many of the world's best wines, and many critics treat the classified growths of Bordeaux from the Médoc and Graves as the gold standard of a proper wine education. So much Bordeaux red is made that in top vintages the quality distinctions between the best wines in each category narrow and there is far more affordable Bordeaux on the market than Burgundy can offer when that much smaller region enjoys a stirling vintage. Besides, Burgundy is far more expensive and generally is riskier.

First and foremost, look for wines from the best estates in the Bordeaux communes of St. Estèphe (red), St.-Julien (red), Margaux (red), Pauillac (red), Graves (mainly Pessac-Léognan, red and white), as well as from St.-Émilion (red), Pomerol (red), Barsac (white, dry and sweet), Sauternes (white, dry and sweet).

When you drink Bordeaux reds, almost always you drink blends, primarily of cabernet sauvignon, merlot and cabernet franc grapes; sometimes petit verdot and malbec play secondary roles. The whites tend to be blends of sauvignon blanc and sémillon.

A basic document that should be at every Bordeaux lover's elbow is the 1855 classification of the region's greatest chateaus, numbering 61. It breaks them down to First, Second, Third, Fourth and Fifth Growths. In many instances, the estates' standards relative to one another have changed, but the general thrust of the categories remains trustworthy.

By the same token, the estates in the 1955 classification of St.-Émilion (updated since then) should be at the other elbow. (There is no formal classification of Pomerol.)

Wines from the topmost chateaus in outstanding vintages need minimally a decade to come around. Several hundred chateaus are found in a category known as Cru Bourgeois. Because they lie outside the golden 1855 circle, they are given short shrift; this is a shame, because some of the best buys for both short- and medium-term (five years) drinking are regularly found in this category these days.

Many estates have second labels (for example, Château Latour's is Les Forts de Latour and Château Haut-Brion's is Bahans Haut-Brion); these wines do not rise to the level of their grands vins, are less expensive but can have long lives and be standout values.

Unlike red Bordeaux, red Burgundy (Bourgogne in French) is a one-grape wine: pinot noir. White Burgundy is entirely chardonnay-based. This makes wines much more responsive to vintage conditions, because the opportunities for blending that can enhance strengths and disguise flaws are limited.

The principal wine-producing areas of Burgundy are the Côte d'Or, which consists of Côte de Nuits, in the north and famous for reds, and Côte de Beaune, in the south and famous for reds and whites. Importantly, Burgundy also embraces

the Chablis and Beaujolais regions. All contribute wines from A-list communes and vineyards that long to sleep in cellars.

Prepare to part with a lot of money. Prepare, too, to run a risk that the pinot noirs, especially, may in the end disappoint you. The pinot noir grape, highly responsive to its soils and surroundings (the complex is called "terroir" in France), and to the winemaker's cellar abilities, is almost, as yesterday's classical Freudians might have said, neurasthenic. When it's good, it sublime, incomparable really; when it's poor, you could cry.

The age-worthy wines come from Grand Cru vineyards, which number more than 30, and Premier Cru vineyards, which exceed 400. I have never encountered anyone who knows the names of all of them, and do not expect to. Unlike Bordeaux's vineyards, Burgundy's do not yield oceans of wines.

The best way to grapple with Bourgogne's complexities is to approach them with the same zest you had for learning baseball batting averages when you were a kid, and the same seat-of-the-pants application you brought to studying for your bachelor's degree. Learn the key villages and a fat handful of the names of their best vineyards for reds. In the Côte de Nuits, those villages are Fixin, Gevrey-Chambertin, Morey-St.-Denis, Chambolle-Musigny, Vougeot, Flagey-Échézeaux, Vosne-Romanée and Nuits-St.-Georges. In the Côte de Beaune, the villages are Aloxe-Corton, Beaune, Pommard and Volnay.

For whites, in the Côte de Beaune, learn Aloxe-Carton, Beaune, Meursault, Puligny-Montrachet and Chassagne-Montrachet.

(Champagne is discussed elsewhere in this book.)

Wine literature is rich in citations of the singular vineyards and—no less important—the names of the most dependable shippers whose labels can be found across America.

In the Rhône Valley, medium-and longer-term reds to seek out are found in Châteauneuf-du-Pape, Hermitage and Crozes-Hermitage; the white appellations are Condrieu and Château Grillet.

Laying down Italian wines is a somewhat less daunting task, though the proliferation of splendid reds makes selectivity difficult if you are on a disciplined budget. Primarily, think Piedmont (Piemonte in Italian), and, particularly, Barolo and Barbaresco. Made from the nebbiolo grape, these are big, fat, muscular, robust, demanding wines that take five to 10 years to evolve. Traditionalist estates make versions that take forever to mature, modernists turn out versions that are drinkable fairly early; no matter which style you prefer, in Piedmont, as in Burgundy, you must be careful to ferret out the best (and often costliest) producers. The same is true of Brunello di Montalcino, from Tuscany, which has such staying power that a magnum from a profound vintage could probably be stored until the Messiah comes. And if you have a taste for the so-called super-Tuscans—the big, expensive, often oaky reds made with sangiovese grapes and international grape varieties (I tend to find them overbearing)—by all means stow away a few to see how they mature.

A cellar partly dedicated to staying power needs rieslings from Germany, especially from the Mosel-Saar-Ruwer and Rheingau regions, both dry and sweet, as well as rieslings and gewürztraminers from Alsace, in northeastern France, and rieslings and grüner veltliners from the Wachau region of Austria.

Assessing Spain's wine spectrum and wine future is difficult but exciting. New regions are emerging, assertive wines made with international grapes are demonstrating powerful drawing power—in short, a revolution is underway across the country. The reds from Rioja, Ribera del Duero and Priorat are the big draw, but heads are being turned by reds from Jumilla and Toro, as well as whites from Rueda. (Don't forget sherry, from Jerez, and, from Portugal, both vintage port and Madeira.)

Thinking of Spain, I am somehow reminded of those astute restaurant proprietors in France during the Impressionist period who smartly accepted young artists' offerings of paintings and drawings as payment in kind for meals they could not afford. The artworks, covering Parisian walls, escalated in value as the artists' reputations grew and spread. Similarly, insightful collectors today might invest fruitful hours buying and tasting new Spanish wines in hopes of fixing on relatively unknown bodegas that one day, perhaps soon, might be comers. If I had the time, I'd do it myself.

As for California, the major auction traffic is in cabernet sauvignons from the Napa Valley (especially the so-called cult wines, which have commanded astronomical—some would say outlandish—sums), Sonoma Valley, Alexander Valley and Santa Cruz Mountains. Pinot noirs from the Russian River Valley, Carneros, and Santa Barbara County invite careful investigation as potential investments, as do Napa and Sonoma chardonnays.

And to make life sweeter, you must lay in a supply of Tokaji, the dessert wine from Hungary.

Filling Your First Bins

One of the best ways to achieve sure footing in your early days of learning about wine is to attend wine classes given by credentialed teachers. Harriet Lembeck has been one of New York City's favorites for 27 years. She runs her own school, the Wine & Spirits Program (formerly at the Waldorf-Astoria Hotel and now in a historic clapboard house in Manhattan); is wine director for The New School University; and is author of *Grossman's Guide to Wines, Beers, and Spirits* (Wiley, seventh edition, 1983).

Knowing that Mrs. Lembeck and I have always been on the same tasting beam—insofar as it is possible, our preferences and interests coincide—I asked her to provide guidance in selecting a startup cellar. Here is her advice:

"The best way to learn which wines to buy, of course, is to taste, especially by making comparisons. I have observed that most people can get into wine comprehension by noting similarities and differences in a small grouping. It is important to find a friendly and knowledgeable wine merchant to support you in your venture.

"Look at white wines and their flavor types. Many whites are similar, even when made from different grapes from different places, often made in stainless steel and not oak-aged. They are less complex and generally best when drunk very young and fresh. A dominant note in their flavors is apples, which is not surprising since one of the acids in wine is malic, an acid also found in apples, even in those as different as a pale Greening and a ripe red Macintosh.

"Compare an albariño from Rias Baixas in northwestern Spain; a pinot grigio from one of the best areas in Italy, the hills (colli) of Friuli; an Austrian grüner veltliner; and a vernaccia from Tuscany, which is apple-like but with overtones of honey.

"For another comparative tasting that requires more careful attention, try a dry riesling from Alsace, France (apple-like with a touch of oak) and a New Zealand sauvignon blanc, which may also have a touch of oak but tends more toward grapefruit flavor. (Many consumers also find a so-called green or herbal character in sauvignon blancs.) A good illustration of a crisp, herbal, no-oak flavor can be found in Sancerre, from the Loire Valley in France. Sauvignon blancs from California are often softened by the addition of sémillon, with brief time in oak.

"Try comparing a Chablis that says only 'Chablis' on the label—indicating only that it comes from the Chablis region of France—with a Chablis from a single vineyard in that region (for example, Blanchot or Fourchaume). Both are made from the popular chardonnay grape, have firm acidity and mineral notes, but the single-vineyard wine will have a more persistent aftertaste and greater concentration. This difference will also help you understand the steps in the French system of wine laws known as Appellation Contrôlée (controlled place names) and also explain the increase in price. (French appellations designate the geographical origins of wines and types of wine, and guarantee that you get what you ask for, but they do not control the quality within those types. For quality, you should rely on well-known producers and on merchants.)

"Add a moderate- to high-priced California chardonnay to the comparative tasting with Chablis, and you will experience more oak, some flavors of tropical fruit, higher alcohol and a greater sense of weight in the mouth.

"To appreciate differences in reds, try a young, probably astringent California cabernet sauvignon, a softer French merlot, a fruity Argentine malbec and a tart cabernet franc from Long Island. Then, thinking of these wines as components in a blend, taste a similar blend in a medium-priced bottle from a Bordeaux chateau, and see if you can recognize the individual strands.

"French Burgundies, on the other hand, are unblended, made from the more delicate pinot noir grape. They can be very costly. Oregon pinot noirs are generally more fruity and less expensive, but many are now coming to market with higher price tags.

"Winemaking methods come into play, too. Compare a soft, light Valpolicella from the Veneto in Italy with a full, robust intensely fruity Amarone della Valpolicella, made from the best grapes, which are dried indoors for about three months before being vinified into dry higher-alcohol wines that benefit from aging. For even more oaky flavors from long oak aging, but with a comparable drop in fruitiness, try a Spanish Rioja gran reserva, a wine that is required to have two years in wood after three years in bottle before release. Note: reserve, riserva, and reserve all have different meanings in different countries. Here's where you need to study.

"And, in the dessert-wine world, try rieslings and sauvignon blanc/sémillon blends. Look for labels that say 'botrytis' or 'late harvest.' The idea is to concentrate the sugar in the grape so that after fermentation there is still sugar remaining in the wine. These are luscious, and can be desserts in themselves. They often come in half-bottles (375 milliliters).

"Once you have become familiar with these broad outlines step by step, it will be time to explore further. It is important to think about flavors, form an opinion and keep detailed notes. Whether you like a wine or not, try to figure out why it impressed you or didn't.

"Use these tasting groups as a springboard to less familiar wine regions. After red Bordeaux, try cabernet sauvignons from Washington State. Portugal has terrific table wines in addition to their famous fortified ports. Don't overlook the Southern Hemisphere. There are delicious wines available from Australia, Chile and South Africa in all price ranges.

"In the end, you will achieve a cellar that reflects you and your judgment."

A Man Who Gets It Right

Willie Gluckstern is not your garden-variety wine professional. For one thing, he got married in the cheese department of Fairway, a you-can-find-everything Broadway supermarket on Manhattan's Upper West Side. For another, his fire-and-brimstone paperback, *The Wine Avenger*, declares up front: "I am a nonlistener to wine talk and a nonbeliever of wine publicists. 'Shut up and put it in the glass,' I say. I'm difficult, I admit it."

While irreverent, iconoclastic and, no surprise, sometimes undiplomatic, Willie is usually right. Right about which wines—he specializes in those from cool climates—are good, and why. If I needed to buy the right wine for the right occasion fast, I know that in five minutes I could find it in his portfolio. The clue to his value system lies in the name on his business card: Wines for Food, a company that imports and distributes wines.

Write to me, Willie, I said. (He was in Deidesheim, Germany, in the Pfalz region, his wife's home, at the time.) Tell me what to buy and why. He replied:

"While big, succulent whites and deep, manly reds remain a traditional staple for drinking and cellaring, acquisition of them has become a kind of discretionary no-brainer, with gospel-like numerical ratings and winery public-relations executives turning the wine-buying public into by-the-numbers zombies.

"For those who prefer clear, appetizing wines that highlight true food flavors over high-alcohol oak-saturated dreadnoughts that submerge all flavor nuance in their turbulent wake, the selection of modestly priced, food-friendly wines for everyday drinking is a piece of cake.

"A purchasing formula for both white and red wines that works well with nearly every meal you can imagine is a wonder of simplicity: look for light- to medium-bodied wines with snappy, cool-climate acidity; for alcohol levels of 12.5 percent or less; and zero exposure to oak of any kind in white wines. Red wines that have enjoyed a relatively brief sojourn in oak (old or new) can still work well with many foods, especially with red meat dishes.

"As an appetite-sharpening prelude to any meal, sparkling wine should be an essential ingredient. Purchase these wines in a shop with high sparkling-wine turnover, as most sparkling wines have a serviceable life span of a year or less from the time they arrive in local markets. Prosecco, the Veneto's crisp, fizzy gift

to gastronomy, is a must. So is earthy Spanish cava (sparkling wine). Chenin-blanc-based Loire mousseux (sparkling) and Deutsche sekt (German sparkling) are also inspired choices to serve before, during or after meals; both are somewhat rare but worth seeking out.

"Some of my favorite still white wines for serving as aperitifs and with all manner of appetizers, salads and seafood include fresh, delicate whites from northern Italy, like early spring releases of young, quaffable Bianco di Custoza from Veneto's Sommacampagna commune; bright and minerally hillside-grown pinot bianco from the Germanic Alto Adige (also known as South Tyrol); and anise- and almond-scented verdicchio from the Marches, a wine of real character, a carafe of which makes a compelling accompaniment to freshly caught fish from the nearby Adriatic.

"From the Loire region in France, herb-scented sauvignon blancs from the vineyards of Sancerre and Pouilly-Fumé; bracing Muscadet, redolent of shell and limestone (a briny oyster's soul mate); the wines of this planet's definitive chenin blanc vineyards, those of Vouvray, Montlouis and Savennières (grownup white wines for gourmands). From Galicia, in northern Spain, there is citrus-tinged albariño, born to join a perfect, local seafood salad. Then there's brash, flashy, olive-scented sauvignon blanc from New Zealand's cool South Island, which is more than a match for the rowdiest seafood and salads. Last, but certainly not least, is Austria's remarkable indigenous food partner, grüner veltliner, at last gaining appropriate access to the United States market and, finally, dry (trocken) German rieslings and pinot blancs (weissburgunders), wines I believe to be the most superlative and versatile with food of all.

"As with sparkling wines, the rule 'the younger, the better' is essential with nearly all white wines, except rieslings and chenin blancs, which, owing to superior acidity, can age beautifully.

"As for red wines, all under $10, my first choices are well-balanced medium-weight wines from Italy, like sweet, juicy, unwooded Barbera from Piemonte; sangiovese from Emilia-Romagna and Tuscany; and inexplicably hard-to-find well-made Bardolino, the quintessential Italian picnic red.

"From France, I tend to favor noncabernet wines, especially syrah-based wines from the Rhône Valley, the sun-drenched Languedoc and France's sprawling southwest; herbal, raspberry-scented cabernet franc wines from Loire vineyards like Saumur and Chinon (in good vintages only); and ripe, juicy Beaujolais, which are indispensable with Hunan, Szechuan and myriad Indian curries.

"Ultra-fun Beaujolais nouveau is a wonderful fruit bomb that detonates on the third Thursday of November each year, just in time to administer suitably to Thanksgiving's plethora of sweet side dishes. Though it burns with a bright light in its youth, nouveau has a life expectancy of only about six months and should be drunk up before that time.

"Here are things you should know that your mother never told you: First, cabernet sauvignon is a gorilla that should be kept securely caged up around anything but red meat. Second, pinot noir that tastes even remotely like it's supposed to at anywhere near even $20 a bottle is pure fantasy. (Buy a savings bond, instead.) Third, white wines are more versatile with far more foods than red wines—no kidding. Fourth, white wines taste metallic with the dark, gray, oily parts of steak fish (bluefish, tuna and salmon). Red wines taste metallic with vinegar (salad dressings), shellfish and snails.

"Remember this easy tip for knowing a great food wine when you taste one: within six seconds after a sip, the taste of the dish should re-emerge as the predominant flavor in your mouth. It's really that simple."

Bubbles

Kurt Eckert was wine director at Jean Georges, the four-star Manhattan restaurant, and Jean-George Vongerichten's other restaurants. He is now Champagne Krug's representative in the United States. I asked about his philosophy of storing Champagne and other wines.

Here's what he said:

"I prefer to consider the storage of Champagne in much the same manner one approaches the storage of any wine of reasonable quality. Wine is a living thing and deserves the best chance for a flavorful evolution. Perhaps it is a result of having had to look after large and diverse collections of wines in fairly constrained spaces that a certain uniformity has taken hold in my cellar practices. It has made me a stickler about eliminating the obvious hazards to wine. All the customary advice is correct, such as maintaining relatively constant low temperature (54 degrees to 56 degrees Fahrenheit) and high humidity (60 percent to 70 percent), and avoiding light and vibration.

"Like any other wine, Champagne should be stored on its side if at all possible. Champagne corks are still cork, and as such they are susceptible to all of the usual cork-related ills, including drying. Try to avoid keeping bottles in the refrigerator for extended periods of time, as they can acquire some rather unusual food-based aromas.

"When is a Champagne at its 'peak'? That depends entirely upon what one wants from the wine. Most contemporary drinkers prefer younger flavors in wine—that is, forward primary fruit flavors, perhaps some apparent oak influence, and a direct, fresh presence. For this group of consumers, wines should be enjoyed

fairly soon after release. More experienced, or traditional, consumers prefer the flavors of aged wines (the so-called goût anglais, or English taste), which emphasize mature secondary flavors, well-integrated acidity, softer textures and perhaps a more evolved appearance. Neither is incorrect. There are no wrong reasons for liking a wine. Storing wine properly allows us to experience a wine at various points along its developmental time line.

"The vast majority of nonvintage Champagnes being sold are perfectly ready to be consumed upon release. They are straightforward expressions of a house style. In most cases, the best components have been diverted into age-worthy prestige cuvées, leaving the 'regular' Champagne with slightly lower-quality ingredients. As with all wines, the overall quality and aging potential depends on what goes into the bottle. The higher the quality of raw material, in the form of rigorously selected wines from highest quality vineyards, the brighter the future potential of the Champagne. The obvious example here is the Grande Cuvée from Krug. This multivintage Champagne is composed of elements from the best sites, growers and vintages and is delightful upon release, yet will age for years and years.

"Too often Champagne is thought of only as an 'occasion' wine, for celebrations or receptions. This deprives us of one of life's great pleasures, namely that of enjoying different types of Champagne with various foods. Champagne comes in a range of styles, from the most delicate to extremely robust. Acquiring some familiarity with various producers and their particular interpretations of the Champagne terroir will open up innumerable opportunities for inventive food and wine experiences."

The Champagne story does not end there. Opening a bottle can be a challenge. One test of seasoned Champagne drinkers is their ability to open a bottle without flinching. The last thing you want is for the cage and cork to fly off, possibly causing injury or damage, and Champagne to leap out of the bottle onto guests and the furniture.

Opening Champagne properly—meaning unobtrusively—is an art. I have never seen a restaurant wine director open one more deftly than Karen King of the Union Square Cafe in Manhattan, which for years has ranked at the top of the Zagat Survey.

"When serving Champagne or sparkling wine, one needs to take special care," she said. "The cork could fly out and hit someone or something. It is very important to pay attention and open the bottle safely.

"When I pick up the bottle, I make sure it is at the proper temperature. Sparkling wines should be served at about 40 degrees Fahrenheit. If the wine is too warm, it expands (since it is bottled under pressure), and the cork could blow out of the bottle.

"The bottle needs to be clean and dry," Ms. King continued. "Maintaining a secure grip on the bottle when you open it is imperative." On the verge of opening it, she said, "I take stock of where I am in the room so that I can point the neck in a direction that has a clear trajectory, so that on the off-chance that something goes awry, the cork will not hit someone."

Without frame-by-frame photographs, King's motions are difficult to convey, but this is the essence of a crucial part of the maneuver:

"I put my left thumb on the foil-covered cork, holding it down securely as I cut the foil with (ideally) two cuts, one clockwise and one counter-clockwise, both under the bottom of the cage. I use my knife to help peel off the foil. The only time I do not have my thumb on the cork is the moment I take the foil off and put it in my pocket along with my knife. The left thumb is immediately back on the cage-covered cork as I start undoing the cage by first twisting its side wire with my right hand.

"Once the cage is worked loose, I put my right hand firmly over the caged cork and grab the base of the bottle. The bottle is turned about six times with the left hand from the bottom. I hold the cork very hard, and as I feel the cork pushing out I may rock it a bit to help let out the pressure slowly. The sound should not be a loud pop but rather a so-called angel's sigh.

"Once the bottle is opened, I take off the cage, put it in my pocket with my right hand. With the bottle in my left hand, I put the cork away, take a napkin with my right hand and gingerly wipe the top of the bottle. I switch the napkin into my left hand and, voilà, I am ready to pour a taste to assure the wine's soundness. In pouring for the table, the wine levels should be equal in all of the glasses. I do not overpour. After the pouring, the bottle goes into an ice bucket with a cloth draped over the bucket so you can wipe the wet bottle before serving refills."

Ordering Wine in Restaurants

For entry-level enthusiasts and even graying wine aficionados, ordering from restaurant wine lists has become exceedingly burdensome and frustrating. There are so many old and emerging wine countries, so many regions and subregions, so many wineries, so many vintages and their variations, so many styles that no one can keep abreast of them.

Sticking with old standbys may be gratifying, but it's hardly educational, and it certainly flies in the face of my own philosophy of trying everything in sight: No two wines are alike, and every next one opened is a potential adventure in discovery.

Thus, in restaurants where I know or trust the sommeliers, increasingly I put myself in their hands by asking them to bring out wines in particular price ranges that exhibit certain characteristics, which I enumerate: for example, full-blown fruit, subtle nuances, fresh acidity. This puts their professionalism to the test, and invariably they deliver the right goods.

Even professionals need helping hands. Mark Bittman, who writes about food for the Dining section of *The New York Times* and is the author of *How to Cook Everything*, and I have trodden the same paths in restaurants. Coincidentally, we did the same thing at separate times at an elegant new Italian restaurant, L'Impero, on the East Side of Manhattan.

We asked the sommelier and part owner, Chris Cannon, for fruity reds within certain dollar ranges, and both of us possibly received and thoroughly enjoyed the same pinot nero from Friuli.

Those handy vintage charts that people used to carry in wallets are barely useful these days. They never were, and never can be, fully authoritative because their symbols—numbers, stars, bottles, whatever—can give only a general slant on a region. No known system can embrace all the permutations of a vintage.

What may be true in one Burgundy vineyard may not be true in the one immediately adjacent. What may be true in the Mosel-Saar-Ruwer region of Germany may not be true in the Rheingau, a few miles away, and in the Pfalz, in another direction.

In short, vintage charts are not gospel.

Neither is reputation. There is no Authority when it comes to taste. Except yourself. Trust your own instincts, needs, judgments and preferences in deciding what to buy in restaurant and what deserves to be in your cellar. Over time—but not overnight—with steady tasting, drinking and thinking, it all sorts itself out.